SUNBEAM MOTOR CYCLES

Motor Cycle Maintenance and Repair Series

Advisory Editor : J. EARNEY

SUNBEAM
MOTOR CYCLES

By
D. W. MUNRO
M.I.Mech.E. M.S.I.A.

WITH THIRTY-SEVEN ILLUSTRATIONS

LONDON
C. ARTHUR PEARSON LIMITED
TOWER HOUSE, SOUTHAMPTON STREET
STRAND, W.C.2

First Published November 1954

This edition published 2017 by
classicmotorcyclemanuals.com
5 Quarry Lane
South Shields
NE34 7NJ

0191 435 4122
www.classicmotorcyclemanuals.com

ISBN 978-1-908890-19-1

Reprinted by
Biddles Books, King's Lynn, Norfolk PE32 1SF

PREFACE

THIS book contains all the information required by the owner or garage-mechanic for the maintenance and repair of Sunbeam Twin motor cycles. It covers Sunbeam types S7, S8 and S7 de luxe.

The opening chapter gives a brief history of the Sunbeam Motor Cycle from the time of its introduction by John Marston to its acquisition by the B.S.A. Co., Ltd.

The various modifications which have been made to the Sunbeam from 1946 up to the present day are outlined in Chapter III, and certain experimental features which were included on the early S7 machines are also fully covered.

Technical data for engine, carburetter and electrical equipment are given in Chapter IV, and data for transmission, sparking plugs and tyres in Chapter V.

Chapter VII of the book deals with maintenance and, for convenience of reference, a table of Regular and Periodic Maintenance requirements is included. Dismantling, reassembly and rectification of faults are dealt with in Chapter VIII, and a list of the proper Service Tools is given at the end of the book.

The author wishes to thank the Sunbeam Division of Messrs. B.S.A. Motor Cycles, Ltd., for providing technical information, photographs and particulars of Service Tools given in this book.

D. W. M.

CHAPTER I

THE SUNBEAM TRADITION

IT is seldom that a new motor cycle has aroused so much interest or evoked so much controversy as did the new twin-cylinder Sunbeam when it was announced in the spring of 1946. True, its appearance came as a complete surprise to the motor-cycling public, starved of technical stimulus in motor-cycling matters after the war years, and as yet not fully conscious of the era of peace which had begun to dawn. And its very novelty was thrown into sharper relief in the mind's eye of that same section of the community by the brevity of the interval which had elapsed since the end of hostilities had allowed the trade to begin setting its home in peacetime order, for most of the post-war motor cycles announced prior to this had been either wartime models finished in black and silver, instead of Service Green, or pre-war types re-introduced as stop-gaps pending the completion of new manufacturing programmes.

In a word, the Sunbeam Twin was one of the first of the genuine post-war designs, and now after a period of several years it is still a model of outstanding design and construction.

But to understand fully the importance of this Sunbeam motor cycle—its impact on the world market, its high place in the order of motor-cycling affairs—it is necessary to look beyond that week in March 1946 when it was first described in the technical Press. We must consider its background, or, if you prefer the term, its antecedents, and those other qualities which have always been associated

FIG. 1.—MODEL S7 SUNBEAM MOTOR CYCLE.

FIG. 1(*a*).—MODEL S8 SUNBEAM MOTOR CYCLE.

with the name, and which go towards the make-up of that intangible but very real thing, the Sunbeam Tradition.

Aims of the Sunbeam Tradition

This tradition stands first and foremost for quality. When John Marston introduced his first Sunbeam Motor Cycle in the early years of the century, he started off with the idea that in every sphere of human activity, not excluding the manufacture of motor cycles, there is room for the best, and he determined that his products should occupy that position—that they should be unchallenged in quality. Furthermore, he interpreted the word quality in its widest and all-embracing sense, to include design, workmanship, performance, reliability, finish and value for money. He thus set an extremely high standard, and it must have been with pride and satisfaction that he and those associated with him during that entire period which has now become known as the John Marston Days, were able fairly to claim that they never lowered it. When therefore the name was eventually acquired by the Birmingham Small Arms Co., Ltd., those who had known the Sunbeam of old speculated widely as to what the outcome of this transaction might be, and wondered whether the Sunbeam Tradition would be maintained. Their fears, if they really had any, were quickly allayed, and their hopes were confidently renewed when they scanned the pages of technical description and studied the published drawings of the new model.

In the next chapter will be found a full and detailed analysis of the design of the post-war Sunbeam, and even a cursory glance at this—though it will amply repay a second and more thorough reading—will show that the present sponsors of this machine had every intention, right from their original conception of the design, of preserving those attributes on which the Sunbeam

Tradition is founded.   That they should have adopted this policy was a source of gratification to countless Sunbeam enthusiasts the world over: that they have succeeded in carrying it out on a model bearing not the least resemblance in design and specification to the pre-war Sunbeams, and in creating a machine which, while truly modern, yet possesses the same quiet and characteristic dignity, is no mean achievement.

CHAPTER II

THE DESIGN AND LAYOUT OF THE SUNBEAM TWIN

THE Sunbeam is a high-class luxury model, embodying every conceivable refinement designed towards improved motor cycling, but it is still a motor cycle with its tubular frame, wire wheels, handlebars, saddle, footrests, foot gear-change and so on.

Engine

The engine is a monobloc twin-cylinder air-cooled unit with the two cylinders and the crankcase cast in one piece, aluminium alloy being used for this purpose, and replaceable alloy iron liners for the bores. The cylinders are arranged in line-ahead (i.e., one behind the other), and so effective is the design and arrangement of the cooling fins that there is a remarkably uniform distribution of heat between the two cylinders, so that the front cylinder never becomes too cool and the rear cylinder never becomes too hot. The two cylinder heads are also formed in one unit, which is likewise cast in an aluminium alloy, and an austenitic iron is used for the valve-seat inserts, which are shrunk into position. The porting in the cylinder-head block is neatly and efficiently carried out, the two exhaust ports emerging at flange-faces on the offside, while the two inlet ports unite at a single flange-face, to which the carburetter is bolted directly.

Valve Gear

The engine is of the overhead-camshaft type, which means that the camshaft itself is mounted in the cylinder-head block.   It lies fore and aft horizontally, and is driven by a vertical chain running up through a tunnel at the back of the cylinder block from the timing gear.   This chain is kept perpetually in correct adjustment by means of an automatic tensioner.   The cam gear in the cylinder head is enclosed by a neat cast-aluminium cover, which is held in place by three studs and nuts.   If this is removed and we look down on the rocker gear, we find on the near-side the camshaft running fore and aft, and on the offside four valves, also running fore and aft in a single line. Between them, running also in the same direction, is a shaft carrying four rockers, each of which forms the connecting link between one cam and one valve.   This is the layout of the overhead-camshaft valve-operating mechanism, and it will be appreciated that it is simple, straightforward and effective, while at the same time, when the cover is removed, it is extremely accessible.

The valves, two per cylinder, are parallel to each other and inclined to the vertical axis of the engine at a slight angle, which is an essential part of the cylinder-head layout, the latter being designed for high volumetric efficiency on the squish principle.   Adjustment for valve clearance is provided at the valve end of each rocker by means of a screwed pin and lock-nut.   The whole of the overhead-camshaft gear is flooded with oil during running, and more will be said about this in the general description of the lubrication system (see Chapter VI).

At the lower end of the camshaft driving chain we find that the sprocket is directly coupled to a large gear-wheel, which in turn, is driven by a small gear-wheel on the crankshaft, the ratio between these two wheels being the usual two to one, in order that the camshaft itself may run at half engine speed.   From this it will be obvious that the lower and upper camshaft chain sprockets are equal in size.

Reciprocating Parts

The pistons, in aluminium alloy, are available in several compression ratios, 6·5 to 1 being standard for the Home Market. They each have two gas or pressure rings, and below these one slotted scraper oil-control ring about the gudgeon pin, and an additional slotted scraper ring near the bottom of the skirt.

The gudgeon pins, which are of the fully floating type, are held in position by circlips, and they bear directly in the small ends of the aluminium-alloy connecting-rods, whose split big-ends are provided with indium-flashed lead-bronze steel-backed liners, running on the accurately ground crank journals. After prolonged tests lead-bronze has been found to be greatly superior to ordinary white metal, and the diffused flash of the rare indium metal, which is applied as a final operation, facilitates the running-in process and greatly reduces the rate of wear.

The crankshaft itself is a high-grade alloy iron casting incorporating a central bobweight. At its front end it runs in a large deep-groove ball bearing, furnished with a spring-loaded oil-seal gland, while its rear journal operates in a plain lead-bronze bearing of generous proportions, which is fitted to a detachable cast-iron housing securely bolted and accurately located in the rear crankcase wall. This housing also functions as the body of the gear-type oil pump, which is driven by the same half-time pinion on the crankshaft that operates the camshaft drive.

Lubrication

Turning next to the lubrication system, we have already found that the oil pump is located in the rear bearing housing and driven from the crankshaft. The oil supply is carried in a sump bolted to the lower face of the crankcase, and an extension pipe from the pump projects into this and draws oil through a filter element fixed to the gauge filter tray. From the pump the oil is delivered upwards to an annular space surrounding the main bearing, and at this point it divides into two separate streams.

One of these passes through a hole in the bearing itself into an internal annulus, from which it enters a hole in the periphery of the crankshaft into its hollow centre, whence it passes in turn to each of the big-end journals, emerging through radial holes to provide lubrication for the plain big-ends. Thereafter this oil escapes into the crank chamber and eventually returns to the sump through the filter, having first lubricated the cylinder bores by splash. The second stream of oil continues round the annulus surrounding the rear main bearing and passes through vertical passages up to the rear end of the camshaft, which it enters through a radial hole in the rear camshaft journal. This oil then passes along an axial hole through the centre of the camshaft right to the other end, where the front bearing is lubricated. The oil then passes on through a connecting passage to the hollow rocker shaft, which it traverses, escaping through radial holes in the latter into the rocker bearings, in each of which a radial hole is drilled in such a position that the escaping oil is projected on to the point of contact between the rocker and the cam. The oil then accumulates in a well below the camshaft and returns through passages down the camshaft driving-chain tunnel, lubricating the timing gear on its way, and it finally returns to the sump. The capacity of the sump is $3\frac{1}{2}$ pints, and the filler cap, accessibly placed on the nearside of the crankcase, incorporates a dipstick.

Built into the oil-pump housing is a spring-loaded pressure-release valve, which is pre-set to operate at 50 lb. per square inch. This acts as a safeguard for the pump and serves to maintain the pressure in the system at this value at normal running speeds. Also included in the system is a pressure-operated oil switch, which is connected through the electrical system to a green light built into the rear of the headlamp. When the pressure in the lubrication system falls below a certain pre-determined level, the green light is automatically switched on, and serves as a warning to the rider either that his oil supply is exhausted or—a much more remote possibility—that something has gone wrong with the lubrication system. This applies at normal running speeds only, for when the engine is ticking-over the green light may come on in much the same way as the red ignition light does at low speeds, but it goes out when the engine is revved up. This light is wired into the ignition circuit, and thus is ready for operation only when the ignition is switched on.

Clutch

As has already been indicated, the engine and gearbox are built in unit construction. This does not mean that the crankcase and gearbox are machined from a single casting, but rather that they are bolted together in exactly the same way as the vast majority of car engines, with the clutch-bell housing forming part of the gearbox shell, and bolted to the crankcase face. The combined flywheel and clutch is coupled to the rear end of the crankshaft on a substantial taper and secured by a single nut of generous proportions.

The clutch itself is of the dry-plate type with the driven member having two Ferodo rings riveted together, one on each side of it, and the engine power is transmitted to it by two steel plates coupled to the flywheel, the pressure being provided by six coil springs. The output side of the clutch (i.e., the drive to the gearbox from the driven member) takes the form of an internal splined hole in the centre of the latter in which the splines on the gearbox mainshaft engage. Of the two steel plates which drive

B

the clutch-driven member, the one nearer to the flywheel carries the clutch-spring pressure, and clutch withdrawal is secured by pressure of a steel rod through the centre of the clutch mainshaft against this plate. The other end of this rod is operated, through a special ball-thrust racer, by the clutch-actuating lever, Bowden controlled from the handlebar in the usual manner.

The clutch is designed to operate dry, and special oil-seals are provided on the crankshaft and the gearbox mainshaft for this purpose.

Gear-change Mechanism

The primary drive reduction is between the gearbox mainshaft and layshaft, and the intermediate gears are secured by the selection of the appropriate pairs of pinions on these two shafts in the usual manner. Output to the rear wheel is from the rear end of the layshaft, to which a flexible universal joint is attached. Gear changing is by a positive-stop foot gear-change mechanism of ingenious design, which is totally enclosed within the gearbox shell.

The principle of operation is as follows. The mechanism comprises a form of face cam (i.e., a flat disc with cam grooves) which is caused to rotate through a double-acting ratchet mechanism by the foot gear-change pedal. The cam, on rotating, causes the gear-selector forks, which engage in the face cam grooves, to slide fore and aft, and thus brings the appropriate pinions into engagement, as required.

This gear-change mechanism is of the genuine positive-stop variety in the sense that the operating pedal always returns to the same position and that the sequence of gear changes up is secured by repeated downward strokes of the pedal, one for each change, and upward strokes for the consecutive changes to lower gears.

Kick-starter

This is worthy of special mention, for the seemingly curious reason that it is conventional in position and operation! The fact is that the engine and gearbox rotate about an axis parallel to the line of the machine, instead of across it, as most motor cycles do, so that a right-angle drive is necessary for the kick-starter if this is to operate in the normal manner. The mechanism consists of a pair of right-angle skew gears, one on the kick-starter shaft and the other on the gearbox mainshaft, and coupled to it through the usual type of spring-ratchet.

As regards lubrication, the gearbox is self-contained, and a filling orifice at the top and a level plug at the side are provided for this purpose, the capacity of the box being approximately 2 pints.

Shaft Drive

The front end of the driving shaft to the rear wheel is coupled to the gearbox layshaft through a shock-absorbing universal joint with synthetic-rubber flexible elements. At its rear end the shaft is coupled to the worm drive through another universal joint, this time of the Hardy–Spicer type, with needle roller bearings. This is easily accessible immediately in front of the worm-drive casing at the offside of the rear wheel. This casing, which is a substantial aluminium-alloy casting, houses an under-slung steel worm supported on ball-and-roller journal races, and provided with an oil seal at its forward end, while a domed cap on its rear end, bolted to the casing, encloses the end location.

Concentric with the rear-wheel axis, and running on two large-diameter ball races, is a bronze worm-wheel driven by the worm which is immediately under it, and this worm-wheel drives the rear-wheel hub through a coupling, which takes the form of a steel sleeve with a wide peripherally-serrated flange at each end.   The serrations at the larger end engage in internal serrations on the worm-wheel, and those at the other end project through the near side of the worm-gear housing for engagement in internal splines in the wheel hub.

For lubrication of the worm drive there is a filling and inspection cover at the top of the casing and a level plug at the side.   Heavy gear oil is used for lubrication, and the quantity required is approximately ½ pint.

Telescopic Forks

The front suspension system comprises a pair of extremely substantial telescopic forks with an unusually wide spread between the blades, designed to give maximum lateral stability.   In the original design, which was produced for about two years (see Chapter III) the two telescopic fork blades functioned as sliding members only, and the spring was carried in a separate unit mounted midway between them and coupled at its upper end to the steering-head and, at its lower end, to the sliding members of the fork blades through a rigid bridge member which embraces the front mudguard.   Fork rebound was taken up by an auxiliary spring in this suspension unit, which was totally enclosed and lubricated by grease gun. For each of the sliding members in the fork blades two heat-treated bronze bushes are provided, and these were lubricated by a method which was unique as far as motor-cycling practice was concerned, since it consisted of cotton wick packed into the centre of the main tubular blades and thoroughly soaked in oil.   Above each wick there was a small oil reservoir which was sufficient to last for a very considerable mileage.

The type of fork now fitted is described later in this chapter under the heading Model S8 (see pages 24 and 26).

Rear Springing

The rear suspension system is of the spring-loaded plunger variety, one spring unit being mounted at each side of the frame at the rear. The plunger on the near-side carries an extension which forms the lug for the rear-wheel spindle, while the offside plunger extends in the form of a vertical flange to which the worm drive is bolted and into the centre of which the rear spindle is screwed. The suspension springs are totally enclosed within telescopic tubes.

Saddle Mounting (S7)

The spring cradle for the saddle takes the form of a helical compression spring enclosed in a tubular member which is inserted into the top frame tube at the rear, and the saddle undercarriage, which pivots on the frame seat lug, has extension arms which project downwards, linking with a plunger rod which operates the spring unit. The geometry of this system has been very carefully devised, and its efficiency is further enhanced by the provision of three adjustment positions, catering for riders of different weights.

Frame

This is of the full-cradle type, with continuous duplex tubes running downwards from the lower end of the frame lug, and sweeping out horizontally and then slightly up-wards, to terminate in the bottom lugs of the rear-suspension brackets. The back-stays from the seat lug terminate in the top lugs of this bracket. The top member is a single large-diameter tube of generous gauge.

Engine Mounting

In order to absorb the transverse engine vibration, and also to control the torque-reaction effect, a special "floating-power" type of engine support has been adopted, and this is found to be extremely effective throughout the entire speed range. The engine–gearbox unit is actually supported at two points only, these being under the gearbox at the rear and just forward of the front cylinder on a line level with the cylinder-head joint. A line joining these two support points passes diagonally through the engine, and also crosses the centre of gravity, with the result that the out-of-balance absorbing moment is at its maximum. At the two supporting points the contact between power unit and frame is through a substantial rubber block of carefully chosen resiliency.

The provisions of these flexible supports permits of considerable engine movement, and this is controlled at the two ends of what may be called the opposing diagonal (see Fig. 2) when the movement about the line of support is greatest. At each of these points there is a pair of adjustable rubber snubbers, and when the machines are originally assembled at the factory the snubbers are set

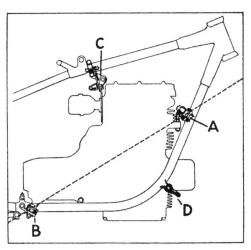

Fig. 2.

Method of Engine Mounting.

A and B, Main pre-set rubber mountings; C, adjustable rubber snubber with vibration damper; D, adjustable rubber snubber.

to give the correct amount of controlled movement. Subsequent adjustment, when it becomes necessary at prolonged intervals, is the responsibility of the owner, and this item is fully described on page 114.

Combined with the upper of the two pairs of snubbers is a high-frequency vibration damper. This is of the spring-loaded friction type, and it is found to eliminate completely the " pins-and-needles " high-frequency effect which is liable to occur on most motor cycles at certain engine speeds.

Wheels and Tyres (S7)

The wheels, which are of the normal wire-spoke type, and fitted with wide well-base rims and large-section tyres, of no less than 4·50 in. for the front and 4·75 in. for the rear. They are also quickly detachable and interchangeable by removal of the spindles only, the rear-wheel drive and brake in the one case, and front-wheel brake in the other, being coupled by splines, as already described.

Coil Ignition

The electrical system comprises coil ignition with a half-engine-speed car-type distributor mounted at the rear of the cylinder-head block and driven by the camshaft. This unit also incorporates automatic ignition advance of the normal centrifugal type. The short high-tension leads to the sparking-plugs are taken through an elegant cast-aluminium sparking-plug cover, bolted to a machined face on the near side of the cylinder-head block. The dynamo is mounted at the front of the crankcase, the armature being connected directly to the crankshaft, and thus running at engine speed. It embodies compensated voltage control, and its output is more than adequate to cover the electrical requirements of the machine.

Silencer

The exhaust system consists of a curved branch pipe, the two legs of which are attached by ring nuts to the two short exhaust junctions, the latter being bolted to the exhaust ports on flange-faces. Below the point at which the two pipes unite, they sweep round horizontally towards a single silencer chamber attached to the lower frame member at the right-hand side of the machine, the connection being through a short length of flexible pipe.

In the silencer fitted to Model S7 there are successive stages of expansion and absorption, which result in an extremely subdued and pleasant exhaust note with a very small power loss. This silencer has been designed in accordance with the very latest scientific principles of noise reduction, and its effectiveness is at once obvious to rider and bystander alike.

The entire exhaust system, being brilliantly chromium plated, adds materially to the handsome appearance of the machine. The silencer of Model S8 is mounted in the same position, and takes the form of an aluminium casting designed to give adequate noise control with the least possible power reduction.

Model S8

In the foregoing paragraphs occasional reference has been made to Model S8, and it is true that, in the main, the technical description forming the bulk of this chapter deals with the original Sunbeam, which was given the title S7. After a run of about two years this was supplemented by a slightly lighter version, to which the name S8 was given, and the original model was continued with the somewhat more ambitious designation of S7 de luxe. This took cognisance of its larger tyres and widely domed mudguards, interchangeable wheels and bolder front forks, for in other respects the specifications of S7 and S8 were identical, apart from the slightly higher compression ratio and freer exhaust used on the latter, which are in keeping with its more sporting character.

From this it will be apparent that certain of the abnormal features of S7 were discarded on S8 in favour of more usual practice, the most conspicuous instance being the standard-section tyres and guards used on the latter.

These two Sunbeam models are now equally established in favour amongst devotees of the marque, the de luxe model being selected by those who must have the greatest possible luxury and are prepared to pay for it, while S8 is for the rider who appreciates the technical specification of the Sunbeam, but is more inclined to assess the value of his mount in terms of windage and overall weight. Although when it comes down to hard facts, there is not a great deal of difference between the two. Be that as it may, Model S7 is certainly the more magnificent motor cycle, but some riders think S8 is more practical.

CHAPTER III

MODIFICATIONS AND IMPROVEMENTS

DURING the six or seven years of its existence the Sunbeam has not undergone any large-scale changes, although numerous modifications, most of them minor, have been made with a view to improving performance or reliability when service and research experience have indicated the desirability of this, or in accordance with the general trend of evolutionary improvement which affects all manufactured articles.

In addition to these, there was the introduction of the supplementary model, S8, to which brief reference has already been made once or twice. Before proceeding with a detailed examination of the nature of the changes which have been made over the years we might profitably give further consideration to this junior partner of the Sunbeam pair at this stage, as it will simplify subsequent reference to certain of the general modifications.

Model S8

This model appeared in March 1949, and while it followed the same basic lines as S7, it differed in the following respects: it is still listed in 1953 as a separate model, and although its specification has been virtually unchanged during this period, one or two of the features which were originally special to it have since been standardised for Model S7 as well. Whenever this applies, a note of it is made in the following analysis.

Engine

The original conception of Model S8 was that it should be a sporting version of the Sunbeam Twin, and it was for this reason that an engine with a slightly higher performance was adopted, this being secured by the fitting of high-compression pistons.

In place of the pressed-in alloy iron liners previously used in the aluminium-alloy cylinder block, a change was made to loose liners. This was arranged simply by an alteration to the fit dimensions and clearances, and in view of the non-symmetrical shape of the combustion heads, it necessitated the provision of locating dowels in the liner flanges, in order to prevent rotation. The adoption of loose liners resulted in a greatly improved freedom from piston slap when the engine reached running temperatures, and it was in fact for this purpose that they were adopted in the first place.

The geometry of the overhead-valve rockers was revised to give, in conjunction with a modified camshaft, an improved action, resulting in smoother operation and reduced wear. The valve timing was, however, not affected at this stage, although it was altered some months later. The actual figures of the old and new timing are on page 39.

Various other detail alterations were made to the engine, most of them dictated by service experience, but as they do not affect service and maintenance in any way it is not considered necessary to deal with them specifically.

Lubrication System

In order to cope adequately with the severer overall working conditions, a modified sump base was employed which increased the oil reservoir capacity by 1 pint, and which resulted in an appreciable diminution of the mean sump temperature.

Superior oil control, and consequently an improved oil consumption, was obtained by the fitting of an additional scraper ring to the piston. There were thus two slotted scraper rings to each piston, in addition to the two normal gas-compression rings. One of these was just above the gudgeon pin in the usual position, and the other was near the bottom of the skirt.

Another item also directed towards oil economy was the adoption of a modified cylinder-head oil-baffle plate. This item is mounted adjacent to the cam and overhead rocker gear, and it is intended to deflect the large volume of oil which is delivered to the cam gear in such a way that it returns to the sump through the special drainage system provided, and does not get drawn into the combustion chambers by way of the valve guides during the induction strokes.

Electrical System

A larger dynamo with a nominal output of 60 watts was adopted. This was interchangeable as regards fitting with the previous one, and resulted in a superior balance of electrical output to meet the requirements of the coil-ignition system, horn, lamps and red and green warning lights for the ignition and lubrication systems respectively.

The wiring diagram, and consequently the wiring harness, was modified to allow for the mounting of the electric horn on the left-hand side of the machine near the battery, instead of on the front down tubes as previously on Model S7. An ordinary dip-switch lever was also fitted to the left handlebar in place of the previous S7 twist-grip operation.

Frame

Basically the frame design was unaltered, but there were one or two modifications worthy of note.

In place of the two pairs of lugs at the rear end for carrying the rear-suspension units, the upper and lower members of each pair being connected by a short length of tube, a single large forged-steel bracket was used at each side.

The ratchet control for the central stand was deleted, and in its place a highly effective roll-up stand was adopted which greatly reduced the effort and skill required to raise the machine. A folding prop stand was also fitted, and this pivoted on an extension to the lug carrying the nearside footrest bracket.

The steering-head lug was modified to accommodate the new front forks fitted. These are described below.

The mudguards, in the case of Model S7 being particularly wide and bold in form, were, and still are, a conspicuous feature of this motor cycle, and indeed one of its principal attractions in the eyes of many owners, quite apart from their high functional efficiency. These wide guards were conceived originally as an integral and essential part of its luxurious specification, matching the extra-large-section tyres adopted. For the slightly more austere Model S8, therefore, they were discarded in favour of narrower guards with tyre sections of the type generally used on motor cycles of this size (i.e., 4-in. rear and $3\frac{1}{4}$-in. front). The styling of the guards, however, and the high finish, which is part of the Sunbeam Tradition discussed in an earlier chapter, were preserved.

On Model S7 the wheels were, and still are, quickly detachable and interchangeable, but although the former feature was retained on S8, the interchangeability was abandoned, and a lighter and simpler hub construction was adopted for a new front wheel designed for accommodation within the new front forks, now to be described.

Front Forks

The first impression gained from an examination of the S8 forks is that they are not as massive as those described in Chapter II; the spread between the legs is considerably less, in keeping with the narrower guard and hub, and the legs themselves appear to be rather more slender. At the same time, the central spring unit placed in the original S7 between the two legs is missing, although this may not be so conspicuous a change, first, because it is not noticeable when the machine is viewed sideways, and in the second place, because this unit is now absent from S7 also.

The S8 forks are thus less rugged than the S7 type, but in this respect appearances are liable to be deceptive, for they are not lacking in strength or rigidity, and in general dimensions and in performance they are at least as good as the best amongst other designs.

Instead of a simple central spring, there is a long helical spring in each leg, and the deflection of these springs under load and road shocks, with a corresponding movement of the sliding fork members, is controlled by an automatic hydraulic damping system, which is progressive in the sense that it offers increased resistance towards the end of the stroke. This is secured by the provision of a reservoir of oil in each fork leg, some of which occupies the annular space between the bushes in which the sliding member moves. As the fork is deflected this annular space becomes less and the oil contained therein, being incompressible, is transferred through specially calibrated holes into the main reservoir. It will be clear that without these holes the forks could not deflect, and also that the rate and speed at which they deflect will be determined by the sizes and positions of the holes. The same factors govern the movement during rebound, for as the space between the bushes increases, the oil is forced back through the controlling holes by atmospheric pressure, and the rate of this transfer controls the rate of rebound. Near the end of the movement in both directions the area of the control holes is abruptly curtailed, and this results in a sharp increase in the damping resistance and a consequently amplified cushioning effect.

Exhaust System

Model S7, being a de luxe machine of refined performance has a pleasantly quiet exhaust note emitted by the highly effective absorption silencer employed. Model S8, on the other hand, partakes of a slightly sporting flavour, and an appropriate silencer was therefore adopted, consisting of a simple cast-aluminium expansion chamber mounted in the standard position and coupled to the standard pipes. This naturally gives a somewhat more energetic exhaust note than the other, but it is nevertheless adequately subdued by modern standards, and it is held by many people to be perfectly in keeping with the nature and character of the model. It probably absorbs slightly less power than the more ambitious design with which the de luxe version is equipped.

Saddle Mounting

A normal three-point fixing for the saddle was adopted for S8 in place of the special sprung cradle which was standardised on the original model, and which is still part of the de luxe specification of Model S7.

Finish

The original Model S7 followed the famous Sunbeam *all-black* practice, and the bold and handsome lines of the machine enabled full advantage to be taken of the brilliant lustre of the enamel, and the high finish imparted to it. This colour scheme, with chromium-plated handlebars, was adopted for Model S8 when it appeared, and a silver-grey polychromatic finish was offered as an alternative.

In view of this it was decided to adopt a new colour for Model S7, and this appeared shortly after the introduction of S8 at the end of March 1949, as a pale greenish or grey tint to be known as mist green. Although at first this was not entirely pleasing to some Sunbeam devotees, who thought only in terms of *all black*, it has since won universal approval.

Miscellaneous Modifications

At the time of the introduction of Model S8, numerous other modifications were made to such items as the fly-wheel, the camshaft-chain tensioner, the worm-driving housing filling orifice and drain plug. All of these were subsequently standardised for both Sunbeam models.

Differences between Models S7 and S8

In addition to those special features of Model S8, to which reference is made in the preceding paragraphs as having since been standardised for both Sunbeam models, it should be noted that the engine specification was also adopted as standard, so that the differences between present-day Sunbeam Models S7 and S8 may be sum-marised in the following table:

	MODEL S7	MODEL S8
Silencer . .	Absorption type, chrom-ium plated	Baffle type, cast alu-minium
Compression ratio (Home Market)	6·5 to 1	6·8 to 1
Wheels . .	Instantly detachable and interchangeable	Instantly detachable
Tyres . .	Front: 4·50–16 ribbed	Front: 2·35–19 stud-ded
	Rear: 4·75–16 studded	Rear: 4·00–18 studded
Brakes . .	8 in. diameter	Front: 7 in. diameter Rear: 8 in. diameter

		MODEL S7	MODEL S8
Saddle	. .	Spring cradle mounting, adjustable for rider's weight	Three-point attachment
Finish	. .	Mist green, with black frame and chromium-plated handlebar, exhaust system, etc.	Black lustre, with chromium-plated handlebar, exhaust pipes, etc. Alternative colour, silver grey

Wick Lubrication

In creating his new model the designer of the post-war Sunbeam incorporated a number of novel ideas, some of which have stood the test of time, while in one or two isolated instances they have been abandoned after a reasonable term of experience.   One of these was the wick lubrication used for three items on Model S7—the front and rear suspension systems, and the spring cradle for the saddle.

This form of lubrication is not by any means new, but its application to certain moving parts of a motor cycle was, to say the least, unusual.   It was abandoned eventually, not because it failed to operate satisfactorily—in fact, it was quite good as far as it went; but it never won the full approval of the motor-cycling world.   It was, perhaps, just outside the ambit of a generation of motor cyclists brought up on oil-cans and grease-guns.   However, there must be many Sunbeam machines on the road at present with wick lubrication at one or more of the three places mentioned above, and there is no particular evidence to show that it is anything but satisfactory.

As the name implies, in this system the lubricant is carried in a reservoir packed with a material performing a function reminiscent of, if not entirely analogous to, the wick of an old-fashioned paraffin lamp.   In the case of the Sunbeam systems this material was of the cotton-wool variety, and the principle was that, in the front-fork legs,

C

the part which normally carries the oil reservoir for the hydraulic damping system—something of the order of $\frac{1}{2}$ pint, as a rule—was packed with cotton-wool, and oil was then poured in and allowed to impregnate through the wool until it was completely saturated. A little more oil was then poured in, forming a reserve supply. In operation the oil oozed out of the wick, making its way to the appropriate bearings, and the quantity thus lost from the wick was replenished from the reserve supply above it, until in due course the latter was all used up—which under normal running conditions might take up to twelve months.

The disadvantage of wick lubrication for the S7 front forks, although an indirect one, was that there was no hydraulic damping—a refinement now considered indispensable for all but the lightest and simplest of telescopic forks. When Model S8 was introduced, with its new forks incorporating the latest form of automatic and progressive hydraulic damping, the wick system naturally disappeared. The forks on Model S7 were subsequently modified in a similar manner, as described later in this chapter.

In the case of the rear suspension, the wick lubrication was perhaps not quite so satisfactory, probably because the amount of deflection in relation to the total dimensions of the suspension columns was higher than in the case of the telescopic front forks. The discharge of lubricant from the wicks was therefore accelerated by actual pressure of impact as well as by capillary action, with the result that excessive leakage occurred, replenishment became necessary at frequent intervals and the presence of oil and accumulated road filth on the external surfaces of the suspension units was undesirable. After a few months of production wick lubrication was therefore replaced by grease nipples.

The third point at which wick lubrication was used was at the saddle cradle, and here again excessive relative movement was doubtless responsible for its abandonment in favour of grease-gun lubrication, although the fact that this wick, being inserted within the top-frame tube, was completely out of sight and therefore out of mind, may have been a contributory reason—a charge which would not hold so firmly when the system was included in the periodical grease-gun routine.

Camshaft-chain Tensioner

As a shaft-drive motor cycle the Sunbeam might easily have been made entirely chainless, but there is one small chain inside the engine, and its extremely important function is to drive the overhead camshaft operating the valve gear.

Like all driving chains, this has a tight side and a slack side during operation, the former due to the pull or tension between the driving sprocket and the one which it drives. If the work or load to which this driven sprocket is coupled is intermittent, as it is in the case of a camshaft opening and closing four valves, then the tension on the tight side of the chain will vary and, again in the present instance, the variation will be from

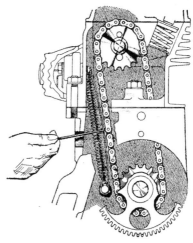

Fig. 3.—Weller Type Chain Tensioner Used on Early Sunbeam Models.

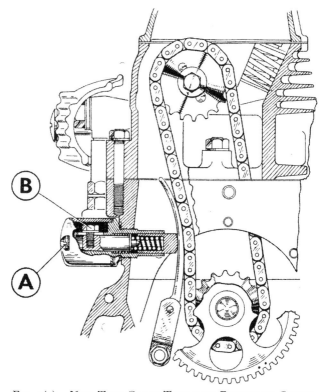

FIG. 3(*a*).—NEW TYPE CHAIN TENSIONER EMBODYING SPRING-
LOADED PIVOTED SLIPPER.
A. Screws.   B. Pinch bolt.

zero to a maximum. This means that at certain times
there is no load on the chain at all, and consequently no
tension. At others we have the maximum tension, as, for
example, when an exhaust valve is being opened against
cylinder-explosion pressure, and at still other times there is
actually a " reversed load " when a valve is closing and the
pressure of its spring pushes the cam round, thus creating

a tendency for the driven sprocket to run ahead of its driver.

It will be evident from all this that the slack side of the chain is important. There must obviously be some slack, for a chain cannot be run dead tight without breaking, but if there is too much the variation in the tension on the tight side will cause snatch and irregularity in the valve timing. Moreover, if this tendency is unchecked it will steadily get worse, for the chain will continually stretch.

This tendency is checked by providing what is called a chain tensioner, which presses against the slack side of the chain, and takes up the play, thus preventing snatch. This tensioner must be able to accommodate itself to wear, and this is done either by periodical adjustment of its setting or, as in the case of the Sunbeam, automatically by spring pressure.

On the earlier Sunbeams the tensioner used was of the Weller type, consisting of a bow-shaped blade of flat spring-steel strip, its ends pulled together by a coil spring, as seen in Fig. 3, and with the periphery of the bow pressing against the slack side of the chain. As the latter stretched due to wear the bow-shaped blade continued to press against the slack side, its radius of curvature changing for this purpose under the pull of the coil spring.

This system, which underwent one or two small detail alterations during its years of use, worked quite well in practice, but under certain conditions it was found to be unreliable, and early in 1951 it was replaced by a new type of tensioner, embodying a spring-loaded pivoted slipper, the operation of which is clearly seen in Fig. 3a.

While not strictly interchangeable with the older system, the new tensioner can be fitted to engines equipped with the earlier type, but the conversion should preferably be carried out by a competent Sunbeam repairer, or at the factory.

S7 De Luxe Forks

The forks fitted to the original S7 with their central spring unit and wick lubrication in the fork legs have been described in Chapter II.

When Model S7 de luxe appeared in May 1949 the central spring and wick lubrication were abandoned, and the mechanical principle of operation employed on the new S8 forks (see page 30) was embodied within the framework of the more massive S7 design, together with the hydraulic damping system also described earlier. The new S7 de luxe front forks were therefore little changed in appearance from the original ones, except for the disappearance of the central spring unit—never very conspicuous in any case—and the appearance of a little chromium plating on the upper portion of each sliding fork leg.   As hydraulically damped telescopic forks, however, they were much more efficient in action than the original type.

Post-war Sunbeam Models

In the following table the history of the various Sunbeam models introduced since the end of the Second World War is briefly summarised:

Model.	Date.	Engine No.	Frame No.
First S7 . .	21.12.46	S7—101	S7—101
Last S7 . .	1.4.49	S7—2371	S7—2205
First S8 . .	25.3.49	S8—104	S8—101
First S7 De Luxe	27.5.49	S8—462	S7—2501

CHAPTER IV

ENGINE, CARBURATION AND ELECTRICAL EQUIPMENT

ENGINE

Technical Data

Cylinder bore	. .	2¾ in. (70 mm.)
Piston stroke	. .	2½ in. (63·5 mm.)
Total capacity	. .	487 c.c. (30 cu. in.)
Compression ratio	. .	6·5 (6·8 or 7·2 to 1 for export or special order)
Ignition timing	. .	Points just opening at T.D.C.
Valve timing (1947–49)	.	I.O. 15° E.
		I.C. 60° L.
		E.O. 55° E.
		E.C. 20° L.
Valve timing (1950–53)	.	I.O. 45° E.
		I.C. 70° L.
		E.O. 65° E.
		E.C. 35° L.
Piston-ring gap	. .	0·004–0·006 in. new
		Max. permissible : 0·020 in.
Piston-skirt clearance	.	With fixed liners 0·0032/0·005 in.
		With loose liners 0·0045/0·0065 in.
Valve clearances (cold)	.	0·018 in.

Note that although the valve-timing figures were considerably altered for 1950, the actual port-opening diagrams were substantially unaffected, the differences in the two sets of figures being accounted for mainly by the slightly modified rocker-cam geometry, to which reference has been made elsewhere in this book, and to revised ideas in the matter of slow-transition opening and closing ramps.

CARBURETTER

Technical Data

Type	Amal 276 CQ/3A (1947–49)
	Amal 276 DO/3A (1950–43)
Choke . . .	$\frac{15}{16}$ in.
Main jet . . .	150
Throttle valve . .	6/3
Needle position . .	2
Needle jet . . .	0·1075

Although there was a change of Type No. for 1950 and later, it will be noted that both the old and the new carburetters bear the same number 276, and this indicates that the carburetter has remained basically unchanged as regards size and class. It will also be observed that the setting, which means jet and choke size, throttle slide, needle position and so on, has also remained constant. In other words, the same type of carburetter has been used throughout on the post-war Sunbeams, but the type number has changed on account of differences in fittings.

Principal amongst these has been the strangler opera-

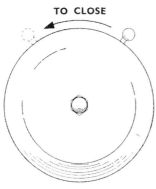

TO CLOSE

tion, and this has been determined by the fitting of the air cleaner. At the time of introduction of Model S8 (see page 38) the Vokes air cleaner was adopted as standard for both Home and Export, and when Model S7 de luxe appeared some two months later this followed suit, with the result that since March 1949 all Sunbeams have been equipped with air cleaners.

FIG. 4.—ORIGINAL CARBURETTER BELL WITH STRANGLER LEVER. Prior to this, only the export

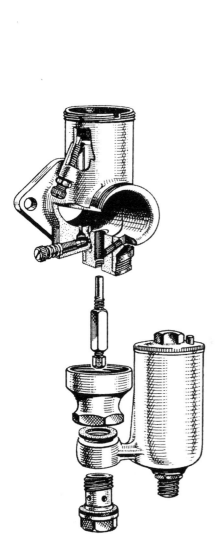

FIG. 5.—EXPLODED VIEW OF THE AMAL CARBURETTER.

Showing spring-loaded plunger attached to air slide in the mixing chamber.

models had this fitment as standard, this being in accordance with the almost universal practice throughout the motor-cycle trade, and as the Amal carburetter on Sunbeams is of the *single-lever* type, this involved a difference in the strangler control for cold starting.

Briefly the position was that in non-air-cleaner models the strangler was operated by a lever immediately behind the bell on the carburetter air intake (Fig. 4), while since there is no such bell on models having an air cleaner, the strangler was replaced by a spring-loaded plunger (Fig. 5) attached directly to an air slide in the carburetter mixing chamber. The operation of these two types of cold-starting device is described further in the riding instructions on page 129.

Carburetter Settings

The important thing to bear in mind is that the settings given above have been devised by the manufacturers in conjunction with the carburetter technical experts after careful tests, and that for normal conditions it is hardly likely that they can be bettered. Note the word normal, however. If the machine is to be used under abnormally strenuous conditions, such as in very mountainous country or continually with a heavily laden sidecar, it may be advantageous to use a slightly richer setting. Conversely, for easy running in level country an appreciable gain in fuel economy may be obtained from a somewhat weaker setting. The only other conditions calling for a departure from the standard setting are high altitudes above sea-level.

The variations in Great Britain and most parts of Europe are insufficient to warrant any change for this reason, but there are extensive regions in South Africa and South America where the mean height above sea-level is sufficient to call for a modification to the setting. The reason for this is, of course, that as the altitude increases the air becomes less dense, and, for a given capacity, less weight of air is induced into the cylinder.   For a correct mixture, therefore, less petrol is required.   In other words, the higher you go above sea-level, the smaller is the jet you require.   As the quantity of combustible mixture is thus inevitably reduced, it follows unfortunately that there will also be a reduction in power.   The following table applies, not only to Sunbeams, but also to all internal-combustion engines.

Height above sea-level in feet.	Reduction in jet size, %.	Approximate power loss, %.
3,000	5	9
6,000	9	18
9,000	13	27
12,000	17	36
15,000	21	45

Permissible Variations in Carburetter Settings

Returning to variations in the standard setting to meet special road conditions, it should be remembered that these must be only slight.   One size up or down on the main jet will have quite a marked effect, and even one notch on the needle position will make an appreciable difference either to performance or to economy.

As a general rule, a change in main jet size has its most marked effect at full throttle, whereas the needle position is more important at intermediate openings.   An intelligent study of the engine performance will often provide the necessary clue, and the following notes will be a useful guide in this direction.

There are several distinct stages or phases in the operation of the carburetter.   There is no sharp dividing line between the successive stage, however, as they merge into each other. They occur at progressive amounts of throttle opening, and we have already hinted at two of these when discussing the relative effects of needle position and main-jet size.

Before investigating the successive stages in their relationship to the variable parts of the carburetter (i.e., those parts which come within the setting category given at the beginning of this section), we should try to get clearly fixed in our minds the idea that the function of a carburetter is to supply a correct mixture to the engine at all speeds, at all throttle openings, at all loads and at all temperatures. Rather a formidable task, and one which, it must be admitted, even the most nearly perfect carburetter fails to perform, although most modern instruments, including the type fitted to the Sunbeam, work very well indeed.

Operation of Carburetter

A carburetter is simply a form of spray-gun, which means that it operates on the same principle as the scent spray, in which a column of air passes over a jet and draws finely divided particles of liquid out of the latter—the liquid in this case being the petrol. These fine particles mingle with the air and, being highly volatile, immediately evaporate, forming a mixture of petrol vapour and air, which finds its way into the cylinder, where it is ignited.

For proper combustion the mixture must be of the correct strength, which under normal conditions is about 17 parts of air to 1 part of petrol vapour. It may be easy enough to get a rudimentary carburetter of the scent-spray type to give this 17 : 1 mixture for a given set of conditions, but to supply it over the whole range of throttle openings is another matter. In any case the 17 : 1 ratio does not remain constant. At low temperatures a richer mixture may be required, as it also is for idling. Again, at high speeds and light loads a weaker mixture may be desirable, while acceleration for any speeds and at any load may be helped by a temporary richening of the mixture.

It is in order to cope with this immensely wide and complicated range of mixture requirements that the modern carburetter has been developed.

Returning now to the successive carburation stages, we might first indicate these in the form of a table.

Stage.	Amount of throttle opening.	Running conditions.	Functional part.
1	Up to $\frac{1}{8}$	Idling	Pilot jet
2	$\frac{1}{8}$ to $\frac{1}{4}$	Acceleration	Throttle slide cut-away
3	$\frac{1}{4}$ to $\frac{3}{4}$	Normal running	Needle jet
4	$\frac{3}{4}$ to full	Maximum performance	Main jet

STAGE 1 : IDLING.—At very small throttle openings very little control comes from the main jet, and the setting of the pilot jet is therefore important. In the Amal carburetter the pilot jet is fixed, and the setting is varied by means of the pilot air screw, which controls the suction on the pilot jet, by metering (i.e., regulating) the amount that mixes with the petrol.

The actual position of the throttle in the " closed " position, which is set for idling or tick-over, is determined by the throttle stop screw, and the following procedure should be observed for correct setting. Loosen the throttle-stop lock-nut and screw the stop downwards until the engine begins to slow down and falter. Then screw the pilot air screw in or out until a position is found where the engine ticks over reliably at a somewhat higher speed. Next lower the throttle-stop screw once more until the engine begins to falter again. Tighten the lock-nut in this position, and finally set the tick-over reliably by further adjustment of the pilot air screw.

STAGE 2 : ACCELERATION.—This is largely determined by the shape of the cut-away on the throttle valve, but it is not likely that Sunbeam owners will have to worry about this item, as it has been carefully selected during the development stages at the factory.

If, however, there is an indication of weakness when the throttle is opened, as evidenced by spitting from the carburetter, this may be cured by slightly richening the pilot setting, which is done by screwing in the pilot air screw about half a turn. If this is not effective, a throttle valve with a smaller cut-away should be tried.

If the carburation appears to be " lumpy ", indicating excessive richness at this stage, then the needle may be lowered a notch. Alternatively, a throttle valve with a larger cut-away may be fitted.

STAGE 3 : NORMAL RUNNING.—The needle controls a wide range of throttle opening as well as acceleration. It should always be used in the lowest practicable position. If the acceleration and the general performance are poor and there are symptoms of weakness, such as a tendency to overheat and pink, especially with inferior fuel, try raising the needle to two notches ! If this gives a marked improvement in performance, lower it one notch (i.e., go back half-way), as this will almost certainly give a superior setting.

Excessive richness, indicated by lumpiness, missing and black smoke in the exhaust at this stage, should be rectified by lowering the needle one or two notches. If the needle is already in the lowest position, then this is an indication that the needle jet is worn and requires replacement. The needle itself seldom wears.

STAGE 4 : MAXIMUM PERFORMANCE.—If you appear to obtain slightly more power on full throttle by easing the twist grip back a trifle, then this is an indication that the main jet is on the small side, and one size larger should be tried. Lumpy, heavy and irregular running, especially if accompanied by a black smoky exhaust, is an indication that the main jet is too large.

Observations made under the paragraph " Plug Reading " on page 61 will also be helpful in obtaining the best carburetter setting.

Note that within the range of jet sizes into which the Sunbeam comes, graduations are in 10's. Thus, as No. 150 is the standard size, then one size larger is 160, and one size smaller is 140.

Maintenance

As a piece of mechanism the carburetter is extremely reliable and trouble-free, and the only attention likely to be required is an occasional inspection to see whether any water and grit have accumulated in the bottom of the float chamber, stripping and cleaning at prolonged intervals and possibly replacement of the main and needle jets after very considerable mileages.

ELECTRICAL EQUIPMENT

Technical Data

Dynamo type . . .	Lucas MC 45 L
Battery	4080050 ; 6 volts, 12 a.h.
Coil	CQO L 11
Distributor . . .	AC 564
Headlamp . . .	8 in. 056452 B
Bulbs :	
Headlamp . . .	6 volts 24/24 watts
Pilot	6 volts 3 watts
Tail	6 volts 3 watts
Stop-tail (when fitted) .	6 volts 3/18 watts index
Oil and ignition warning	
lights	2·5-volt, 0·2-amp. screw type

Notes : 1. The 1947/48 models had a smaller output dynamo.
2. The stop-tail lamp with index bulb is standard for 1953, and available as an extra in previous years.

Battery Maintenance

Unquestionably the most important item in any auto-motive electrical system, and especially so in the case of machines making use of coil ignition, such as the Sunbeam, is the battery, for upon its condition will depend not only the correct functioning of the lighting system but also the running of the engine. Without an adequate supply of current for the ignition system, the engine cannot function properly, and if the battery is badly below par it may make starting difficult or even impossible.

It therefore pays to keep your battery in good condition, and this is really quite a simple matter, calling for no special skill or experience. It merely amounts to giving it a regular inspection, say once a month, or even less if you do big mileages, to check the level of the electrolyte (i.e., the dilute sulphuric acid with which it is filled). This should be just level with, or just a shade above, the separators (i.e., the internal parts of the battery which are visible through the filling-plug holes). If the level has fallen, which it tends to do with the passage of time, it must be made up with *distilled water*. Do not use tap water for this purpose, because the chemicals dissolved in it, which do not, of course, affect its drinking qualities, are harmful to batteries. Another thing: never use a naked light, such as a match, for examining the battery, because hydrogen gas is generated during functioning, and this is highly inflammable, and under certain conditions it may actually be explosive.

Testing Specific Gravity

A useful check for the condition of a battery is to test the specific gravity (density) of the electrolyte, and this may be done with a simple instrument called a hydro-meter, obtainable at any garage. Some owners prefer to purchase one for their own use, but if this is not desired you can always get your garage man to check your battery for you.

The hydrometer gives a direct reading of the specific gravity, and the following figures are given as a guide. They are for a temperature of 60° F., which is about average for this country.

Condition of battery.	Specific gravity of electrolyte.
Fully charged . . .	1·280—1·300
Half discharged . . .	About 2·110
Fully discharged . .	Below 1·150

The readings for each cell should be about the same. If one is much lower than the others, it will indicate internal leakage or a short-circuit in the cell, and the battery should be given expert attention by an authorised service agent.

Never leave a battery for long in a discharged condition, or it will deteriorate and be unfit for subsequent service. When the machine is to be out of action for some time, see that the battery is fully charged, and get your garage to give it a short refreshing charge every fortnight. This will keep it in good condition, and ready for immediate use when the time comes.

Dynamo Maintenance

The only items likely to require attention here are the commutator and brush gear, and these should require inspection only at prolonged intervals—say once or twice a year.

Take off the end cover, which is held by two screws, and check that the brushes are free in their holders.   This can be done by pulling the flexible connectors gently.   If a

D

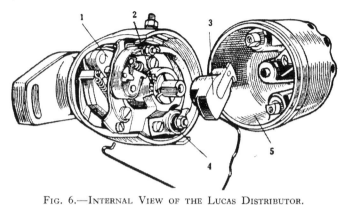

FIG. 6.—INTERNAL VIEW OF THE LUCAS DISTRIBUTOR.
1. Governor weight. 2. Spindle bearing. 3. Rotor. 4. Terminal.
5. Cap.

brush is tight, take it out and clean it with petrol. Be careful to replace it the right way round, or it will not make proper contact on the surface of the commutator.

The commutator should be clean and bright. If it is dirty, clean it by pressing a fine dry duster against it while turning the engine over slowly. If very dirty use a petrol rag. In extreme cases a piece of fine emery cloth may be used, but this is not recommended unless you have some skill in electrical matters.

Distributor and Coil

The distributor comprises three distinct items: the contact-breaker, the distributor proper and the automatic ignition advance.

The last of these is of the centrifugal type, and its slight lubrication requirements are automatically supplied by the engine: it is therefore best left severely alone.

The cam which operates the contact-breaker lever and the pivot on which the latter moves should be given a light smear of grease every few thousand miles. Take care, however, that none of this grease gets on to the contact-breaker points.

Examine the points at similar intervals. If they are burned or charred clean them with fine emery cloth, and wipe carefully with a dry rag before replacing. Check for gap after cleaning. This should be according to the gauge provided on the ignition screw-driver, and is about 0·012–0·015 in. when the points are fully open. If incorrect, slacken the two screws which hold the plate carrying the fixed contact (see Fig. 6) and move this plate until the proper gap is obtained. Then re-tighten the screws.

The only other attention required by the distributor is to see that the small carbon brush in the centre of the cap inside is free in its housing. This is important, since it carries the high-tension current from the coil to the distributor arm, whence it goes to the two sparking-plugs.

COIL.—The coil requires no attention whatsoever, apart from an occasional check that the three wires connected to it are tight at their terminals.

Cut-out and Regulator

These are housed in the control panel, which is mounted adjacent to the toolbox under the saddle. They are entirely automatic in action, and must on no account be interfered with. The correct adjustment of these items, which is carried out by the makers during manufacture, calls for a high degree of skill and experience, and un-authorised tampering will only produce detrimental results.

MAINTENANCE TABLE

The following items should be checked and rectified if necessary at the mileage intervals stated.

After the first 500 *miles*

Check the contact-breaker-points adjustment.

Every 1000 *miles*

Top up the battery.

Every 3000 *miles*

Grease distributor cam lightly. Give a few drops of thin oil to the cam-spindle bearing (having first removed the rotor-arm).

Grease contact-breaker pivot lightly.

Every 6000 *miles*

Clean the distributor thoroughly.
Check the condition of the points.

Every 12,000 *miles*

Examine and clean the dynamo brushes and commutator.

Replace the former if badly worn.

CHAPTER V

TRANSMISSION, SPARKING-PLUGS AND TYRES

TRANSMISSION

Technical Data

Clutch	Single plate, dry
Dia. of clutch plate . .	8 in.
Speed of rotation . .	Engine speed
Primary reduction in top gear	1·39 to 1
Position	Between gearbox mainshaft and layshaft
Final drive . . .	By worm and wheel
Final reduction . . .	Solo, 6 : 23 ; Sidecar, 5 : 22
Overall ratios :	
Solo	5·3, 6·5, 9·0, 14·5
Sidecar . . .	6·13, 7·4, 10·3, 16·6

It will be noted that the change from solo to sidecar gearing calls for special consideration. In the conventional motor cycle with all-chain drive it is customary—although not universal—to change from solo to sidecar gearing, or indeed to make any change in the overall ratio, merely by fitting a new engine-shaft sprocket. Obviously this cannot be done in the case of the Sunbeam, for there is no engine-shaft sprocket, and owing to the design of the gearbox any alteration to the ratios at this point would involve the fitting of an entirely new gear cluster. The change is therefore made at the final drive, which mean that there are two worm and wheel sets : one for solo and one for sidecar.

The fitting of these is unfortunately beyond the scope of the average private owner, and the conversion from solo to sidecar gearing or *vice versa* should be carried out by a competent mechanic or Sunbeam dealer. For the benefit of those who are capable of doing this class of work, some notes on assembly are given on page 115.

When a new machine is ordered in the first place the required gearing is usually specified to the factory by the dealer, on instructions from his customer, and the machine leaves the factory correctly equipped. If not, then the conversion is made before the machine reaches the customer, unless, of course, the latter decides after acquiring the machine to fit a sidecar or to remove his sidecar and run solo.

When a change in final drive is made, it is also necessary to fit a new speedometer drive to the gearbox; otherwise the speedometer will read incorrectly when the change is made. Particulars of the parts required for gear-ratio and speedometer-drive conversion are shown in the following table, the figures given being the manufacturer's part numbers taken from their spares list.

Item.	Solo.	Sidecar.
Worm	89–5521	89–5526
Worm-wheel . . .	89–5520	89–5525
Speedometer driving worm .	89–3060	89–3066
Speedometer driven pinion .	89–3223	89–3067

SPARKING-PLUGS

Technical Data

Plug diameter	.	.	.	.	14 mm.
Reach .	.	.	.	.	Long reach ($\frac{3}{4}$ in.)
Standard Model :					
1947–1952 .	.	.	.	.	Champion NA8
1953 *	.	.	.	.	Champion N8B

* The Champion N8B is also suitable for the earlier models.

The sparking-plugs fitted to Sunbeam motor cycles have been selected by the manufacturers after long and careful tests, and, provided that a machine is otherwise in a satisfactory condition, they should give many thousands of miles of efficient service before replacement eventually becomes necessary or desirable.

If the carburetter is kept in perfect adjustment, the points and the interior of the body should remain clean, and any excessive deposit at these points is an indication that something is out of order. The implications are dealt with more fully under the heading of Plug Reading, and it will therefore suffice to note here that the formation of carbon on the points and inside the body is due either to an excessively rich mixture from the carburetter, or to too much oil reaching the combustion chambers and becoming carbonised under the action of the intense heat generated there during running.

These two types of deposit may be called petrol carbon and oil carbon. The former is usually of a soft, velvety black texture, and is quite easily wiped off. Oil carbon is harder and coarser in structure, and often adheres with considerable tenacity, requiring vigorous action with a pen-knife blade, or other suitable scraping tool, for its removal.

Another kind of deposit that is apt to be troublesome after an extended mileage is due to the use of leaded fuels, but it is only after lengthy periods of running that it makes its presence felt, and it should therefore not be regarded in any sense as a real deterrent against this type of fuel, which has otherwise everything to commend it. This deposit is usually grey or greyish-brown in colour and, besides being very hard, it clings very firmly to the points and inside the body. Like carbon deposit, this by-product of the combustion of leaded fuel has the property of conducting electricity to a slight extent, with the result that when present in excessive quantities it affects the spark, either short-circuiting the high-tension current completely, in which case there is no spark, or weakening the spark, with consequently incomplete combustion and impaired performance.

Cleaning the Plugs

The remedy is obvious in all cases: clean the plug. The Champion Plugs fitted to all Sunbeams are non-detachable, but, even so, it is possible by careful manipulation of a suitable small scraping tool to make quite a good job of the cleaning operation. Preferably, however, they should be taken to your dealer, who is almost certain to be equipped with a special cleaning machine. A few moments' work on this apparatus, at a trifling cost, will restore a plug to its original efficiency.

Adjusting Points Gap

The only other attention a plug is likely to require is periodical examination of the gap at the points. Owing to the high temperature of combustion, which, after all, starts at the points, the latter are subjected to an extremely slow but inevitable process of deterioration. In other words, they gradually burn away, and although it is many thousands of miles before this process reaches a stage at which a plug requires replacement, it nevertheless pays to check the gap at regular intervals—say every 1000 miles—and adjust it when it becomes excessive due to this burning process. This is simply done in the case of the Champion models by bending the side point, either with a special tool as seen in Fig. 7, or in default of this, by gently tapping it with a very light hammer or other suitable object.

The correct gap between the points up to 1953 was 0·015–0·018 in., and for 1954 this has been altered in

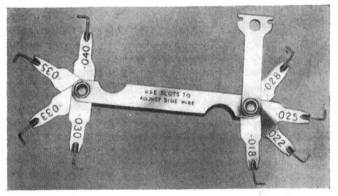

FIG. 7.—SPECIAL TOOL FOR ADJUSTING SPARKING-PLUG POINTS.

accordance with the latest practice to 0·018–0·020 in. This gap can easily be tested with a suitable gauge obtainable from any garage or from the plug manufacturers. The type illustrated in Fig. 7 is a combined gauge and adjusting tool.

The Plug to Use

The primary function of a sparking-plug is to provide a spark for ignition, and the original type, as used in the engines of half a century ago, were, as the name implies, simply plugs of metal screwed into the wall of the combustion chamber in such a way that their central insulated electrical conductors, when supplied with a suitable current, allowed a spark to jump to earth, thereby igniting the mixture.

Questions of gas space, the size, shape and number of electrodes, the dimensions of the insulator and even the materials used probably caused little or no concern to the designers of these early plugs, because all they had to do was to provide a spark, and that was miracle enough for those days.

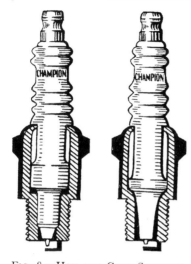

FIG. 8.—HOT AND COLD SPARKING-PLUGS.

(*Left*) Cold plug.   (*Right*) Hot plug.

Nowadays, with the enormous complexity of engine types, we have a wide range of sparking-plugs, all possessing the common function of providing sparks, but otherwise differing considerably in shape, size and design.

Some engines run hot, while others run cool, and though at first glance it may seem curious, it is generally true that the hot engines are those with the lowest combustion temperature, while, conversely, the cool-running types have the highest flame temperature. For this wide diversity in engine performance we naturally require different kinds of plugs. One would not expect the plug used in a low-compression side-valve engine to be suitable for the T.T. races, and the reverse also applies, although even in these enlightened days the fallacy that a " hot " plug will improve the performance of any engine has not quite died out.

The fact is, of course, that there is a *best* plug for every type of engine ; and that the design and character of that plug are governed by the nature of the engine, and more particularly by its heat characteristics. Modern sparking-plugs are, in fact, classified in accordance with their position in what is known as the *Heat Range*, and in present-day parlance they are described as being either *hot* or *cold* (see Fig. 8).

At this stage we must disabuse our minds of the old

conception of a " hot " plug for an engine with a " hot " (i.e., a super sports) performance, the opposite type—for use in low-efficiency units of the side-valve type usually being called " soft ". In an attempt to rationalise the whole position plug and engine manufacturers, in compiling their lists and heat ranges, have assessed the values of sparking-plugs on their ability to withstand combustion or flame temperature, and have placed them in the heat range in accordance with this assessment.

Thus, a plug which because of its high heat resistance is suitable for a high-compression, high-performance engine is placed high on the heat-range scale and is described as a *cold* plug. By the same token, the plug used in a low-compression, low-efficiency engine stands near the bottom of the heat range, and is called a *hot* plug.

In the case of cold plugs the length of the central insulator and the size of the annular gas space are kept as low as possible to keep heat out. There is thus a very small internal area on which carbon may form or oil may be deposited, and the result of this is that cold plugs are very sensitive to oil (i.e., they oil up easily).

Hot plugs warm up quickly, for the insulator area and gas space are large, thus providing plenty of surface to absorb the smaller amount of heat present. This large area also makes internal shorting by carbon or oil more unlikely, with the consequence that hot plugs are much more tolerant to oil. They cannot stand so much heat, however, and if used in an engine for which they are not suitable, they will overheat and the electrodes will become incandescent and burn away rapidly, in the meantime causing pre-ignition and sundry other unpleasant symptoms.

Points to Note when Changing Plugs

A proper appreciation of these remarks will make it clear not only why manufacturers take so much trouble to

FIG. 9.—EFFECT OF OILING-UP ON SPARKING-PLUGS SHOWING
OLD AND NEW PLUGS.

discover the most suitable plugs for their models but also
why the private owner should be very careful when considering a change. He should first satisfy himself that a
change is really necessary. If the engine is running satisfactorily and if the plugs fitted remain in a sound condition
for a reasonable mileage, then there is no need to change
them. If, however, the plugs tend to oil or carbon up,
then a warmer type will be desirable. This is likely
to happen only when the cylinder bores or piston-rings
become badly worn and too much oil is reaching the
combustion chambers. Under these conditions the fitting
of warmer plugs cuts out the oiling-up tendency, but it
can be regarded as a palliative only until such time as a re-
bore becomes possible (see Fig. 9).

If an engine is used for extra high duty, such as continuous high-speed work with a heavily laden sidecar, or
if it is used in difficult mountainous country calling for
long periods of full throttle, it is possible that the standard
plugs fitted may prove a little too warm and cause occa-

sional pre-ignition. In such cases a change to the next model in the heat range (i.e., one stage cooler) may be beneficial, but the owner should remember that this will involve a slightly higher degree of sensitivity to oil and carbon deposit on the plug points and inside the plug bodies.

The following Table gives the appropriate heat-range stages for Sunbeam motor cycles for three well-known brands of sparking plug.

Duty.	Champion.	K.L.G.	Lodge.
Normal . .	NA8 or N8B	FE70 or FE50	HLN or CLN
One stage warmer .	N7	FE20	BL14
One stage colder .	NA10	FE100	3HLN

Plug Reading

A study of the preceding notes will have made it evident that the sparking-plug is one of the most sensitive components of a motor-cycle engine. An examination of its condition and appearance can reveal many secrets to the expert rider, and his ability to read and interpret the story told by his plugs is a most valuable asset, not only for motor cycling as a pleasant pastime, but also for the more serious aspects of trials and sporting events in general.

If the plug fitted is unsuitable—if it is too hot or too cold—it will soon announce the fact by overheating or oiling up, but if the actual model used is known to be suitable for the engine, and for the kind of work the engine has to do, then an inspection of it after even a short amount of running will indicate to the experienced eye the condition and setting of the engine. This inspection is known as plug reading, and is invariably carried out by riders and mechanics during the preparation for any sporting event, as an item of vital importance. It is also recommended as a useful check by the private owner, even though his thoughts may never stray anywhere in a sporting direction.

Of course, any plug can be read, for the condition of the points, the gas-space and the conical insulator for the central electrode will show the state of the engine. The colour and texture of the deposits, if there are any, and the appearance of the metal and porcelain parts will indicate whether the mixture is correct, whether the cylinder needs a re-bore or new rings, how the ignition setting is and so on, but most of these things become self-evident in any case during running by the display of more direct symptoms.

After the preliminary work on ignition setting and carburation has been completed and the engine appears in practice to be just about right, a plug reading should be taken as a final check, in the following manner.

New plugs are fitted and the machine is given a short flat-out run. It is then stopped as quickly as possible, and the plugs rapidly removed and examined. Regardless of how good the performance may be, if the points are absolutely clean, then the mixture is on the weak side, and if they are whitish grey it is dangerously weak. Should the points and the interior of the body be coated with a rich velvety black deposit, no matter how thin and easily wiped off, the indication is that the setting is rather too rich, but the presence of at least some trace of carbon deposit is essential for safety, even though it is so thin that it just lightly stains the points.

The reason for this apparent fuss about the condition of the plug points is that a mixture that is theoretically correct, because it burns completely without leaving any carbon deposit, is not necessarily the best for maximum power, and it is certainly not the safest from the risk of overheating and consequent seizure.

Once having determined the jet size which on a short test shows absolutely clean points, the wise owner will immediately fit one size larger jet. He will then know that his mixture is not too weak, and is, in fact, just a trifle on the rich side to help to keep his engine cool.

The above notes on plug reading are given for the benefit of the enthusiastic and expert rider who takes a particular pride in the condition of his machine. To those who prefer to avoid anything which they consider to come within the category of " tinkering " they are offered as a piece of interesting information, not necessarily to be carried into practical effect. In any case, all Sunbeam owners may rest assured that the makers themselves did quite a lot of plug reading during the development stages, and the standard settings are the result of this work.

TYRES

Technical Data

Model.	S7.		S8.	
	Front.	Rear.	Front.	Rear.
Size . .	4·50–16	4·75–16	3·25–19	4·00–18
Tread . .	Ribbed	Studded	Studded	Studded
Pressure (lb. per square inch) :				
Solo . .	19	19	18	16
Sidecar .	19	19	24	16

The 1947 and some early 1948 S7 machines were fitted with a 4·75–16 front tyre with studded section. Recommended pressure for these was as later models (i.e., 19 lb./square inch).

Notes

1. The studded tread in the above table refers to the Dunlop Universal type.

2. The Sunbeam Sidecar, Model 522/50, which is suitable for both models, is fitted with a 3·50–19 Dunlop

Universal tyre, and the recommended pressure is 16 lb./square inch.

3. The recommended tyre pressures given above are for ten stone (140 lb.) driver and passenger. If these weights are greatly exceeded—say by one stone or more—due allowance must be made for this in the pressures used, or the tyres will develop the symptoms of under-inflation and suffer accordingly. On Model S8 an extra 1 or 2 lb./square inch should be given for heavier driver and passenger. In the case of Model S7 this is perhaps not so important, as the machine, with its abnormally large-section tyre, is more than adequately shod.

When a pillion passenger is carried, particular attention should be given to the rear-tyre pressure. An increase of 2–4 lb./square inch would not be out of place.

Care of Tyres

This is thoroughly dealt with in the literature supplied with the machine, and it should only be necessary here to emphasise one or two of the more important points.

1. Never run in an under-inflated condition. This causes rapid wear and early collapse of the side walls. The amount of extra comfort obtained is very problematical, and more than offset by the increased wear and reduced road safety due to rolling.

2. Over-inflation is also undesirable. It does not help tyre wear appreciably, and it reduces comfort considerably. It is also liable to reduce safety due to bouncing.

3. Examine your tyres periodically for the presence of flints, nails and other foreign bodies which may be embedded in the rubber or wedged between studs. If not removed promptly, these may work eventually their way right through the rubber, damaging the

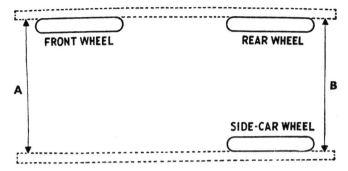

FIG. 10.—CORRECT ALIGNMENT OF MOTOR CYCLE AND SIDECAR.
Dimension A should be equal to B, or up to ⅛ in. less.

fabric and puncturing the tube. This examination is especially important after a run over newly dressed road surfaces.

4. Oil and grease are harmful to rubber, so keep your garage floor clean. If oil or grease has found its way on to the rubber wipe the tyres clean with a rag moistened with petrol, but remember that petrol is also harmful, and only use a little on your rag.

5. If a sidecar is used, see that it is properly lined up with the machine. The cycle should either be vertical or leaning outwards just the merest shade: it should not on any account lean inwards.

Check the alignment of the three wheels as shown in Fig. 10. The dimension A should be equal to B or up to ⅛ in. less. On no account should it be greater than B, or excessive tyre wear will result and steering will be impaired.

6. Remember that neither natural nor synthetic rubber is absolutely air-tight, and that even a perfect inner tube will not hold its pressure for ever. So check your pressures regularly with a gauge. The money spent on one will be a sound investment.

E

CHAPTER VI

THE LUBRICATION SYSTEM

Engine

THE lubrication system employed in the Sunbeam engine is of the wet-sump circulating type, and it thus differs in principle from that used in the majority of present-day motor-cycle power units, since these are of the dry-sump type. This latter term is actually a misnomer, because in most dry-sump systems there is no sump at all, the oil supply being carried in a separate reservoir or tank, usually mounted under the saddle, and connected to the engine by two pipes—one for supply and the other for return. The oil pump in such cases is double, one portion drawing oil from the tank and delivering it under pressure to the appropriate engine parts, while the other portion collects the oil from a well in the crankcase, where it accumulates and returns it to the tank.

In the Sunbeam system (Fig. 11) these complications are reduced to a minimum, and in comparison with the dry-sump principle it is much simpler, although no less efficient. There is no separate oil tank, for instance, the unit is completely innocent of external oil pipes and a single oil pump is adequate to ensure the correct functioning of the system.

The system is called *wet sump* for the entirely satisfactory reason that the sump is, in fact, wet, for it carries the oil supply. The lower part of the sump is detachable, being bolted to the bottom face of the crankcase, and this is a great convenience for maintenance and other purposes.

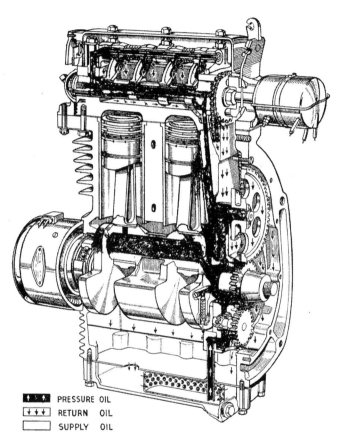

PRESSURE OIL
RETURN OIL
SUPPLY OIL

FIG. 11.—SECTIONAL VIEW OF LUBRICATION SYSTEM.

Showing direction of oil flow. This is a wet-sump circulating system, the oil being contained in the sump.

We shall deal further with this part of the system later in this chapter.

Operation of Oil Pump

The principle of operation is quite straightforward, and is as follows. The oil pump, which comprises a single pair of gears running in a suitable housing machined in the rear crankshaft bearing carrier (see Fig. 23), draws oil through a short suction pipe from the supply in the sump. This pipe projects into a filter mounted in the sump and attached to a conventional tray bolted between the sump and the crankcase. The filter has undergone one or two changes in design since the Sunbeam Twin was introduced, and this point is also dealt with later.

From the pump the oil is forced upwards under pressure to the annular space surrounding the crankshaft rear bearing. Here it divides into two separate streams. One of these passes through a hole drilled in the wall of the bearing, and there it enters an internal groove in the bearing. It provides lubrication for this bearing and then passes through a hole in the crankshaft journal, and thus enters the hollow crankshaft. Passing along to the two big-end journals, it is now forced by the pressure of the pump to the actual big-end bearings, which are of the plain loose-liner type (see page 15).

Having provided the necessary lubrication at these points, the oil then oozes out from between the crank journals and the bearing liners into the crank chamber, where, as it is already in a finely divided condition resulting from its emergence from the close-fitting big-ends, it is immediately churned into mist by the rapidly rotating crankshaft. Some of it is deposited on the cylinder walls, where it lubricates the pistons. The latter are provided with two scraper rings each, and these *wipe* the oil forming on the cylinder walls, and as they operate only during the down-stroke the result is that the oil in liquid form tumbles down into the sump beneath, and this completes its part of the circulating-system cycle.

The second stream of oil formed at the crankshaft main bearing is carried beyond the annular space surrounding this bearing, and travels upwards through a drilled passage in the aluminium wall of the cylinder casting to the cylinder top face, where it then enters a corresponding drilled passage in the cylinder head. From here it is led straight to the rear camshaft bearing. Lubricating the latter, it next enters a radial hole in the camshaft journal, passes along the hollow camshaft to the front end and lubricates the bearing at this point also. The oil stream has not yet reached the end of its journey, however, for it now passes through the bearing with a connecting channel to the valve rocker shaft, which is hollow but closed at its far end. Its only means of escape from the rocker shaft is through four holes in its wall, one drilled radially in line with each of the four valve rockers. These rockers each have a hole in their bearing bosses arranged in such a way that every time they oscillate to open their valves under the action of the camshaft these holes uncover the holes in the rocker shaft. The result is that a momentary and intermittent jet of oil emerges from each rocker, and the holes are so placed that these jets aim directly at the points of contact between cams and rockers, thus providing an effective oil supply where it is most needed. This oil then accumulates in a channel formed in the floor of the cam-box, and it then flows back under the action of gravity down the camshaft driving-chain compartment and finally into the sump.

Points to be Noted

Three points to be noted are, first, that between the oil pump and the camshaft main bearing there is a by-pass spring-loaded ball-release valve. This controls the pressure in the system to not more than 40 lb. per square inch, and thus acts as a safeguard for the pump. The second point is that there is a short by-pass supply leading from the second stream described above to the bearing which carries the half-engine-speed timing pinion. These two items are clearly seen in Fig. 11. The third point is that an electrical contact unit of the diaphragm type is by-passed into the oil-supply line. This operates a green warning light built into the headlamp body and clearly visible from the saddle. The pressure in the system normally keeps the contacts apart so that the light does not shine. If for any reason, such as lack of oil or insufficient engine speed, the oil pressure falls to below a few pounds, the contacts close and the green light comes on. This naturally occurs when the ignition is switched on prior to starting the engine, for under these conditions there is no oil pressure, but as soon as the engine fires the light should go out. It may flicker in and out, or even shine steadily during tick-over, especially if the carburetter is set for very slow running. This is quite normal, but if the light should shine at ordinary running speeds, an immediate stop should be made for investigation. As the Sunbeam is virtually foolproof, there are only one or two likely causes of this:

1. SHORTAGE OF OIL. If the oil supply is allowed to fall below the safe limit, which is about $\frac{1}{2}$ in. below the mark on the dip-stick, the pump will tend to draw air instead of oil, especially over bumpy roads, and the pressure will fall dangerously.

2. RELEASE VALVE STUCK. This is only likely to stick open if the ball is held off its seat by a particle of dirt or foreign matter. This will allow the oil to return straight to the sump without lubricating the engine. The remedy in this case is obvious.

3. BEARING WEAR. Excessive wear at any of the bearings mentioned during the description of the system will allow leakage and loss of pressure. This cannot happen suddenly, however, except in the case of the big-ends, but with modern design and modern bearing materials the old bogey of run big-ends is practically a thing of the past.

Oil Sump

Although strictly speaking the oil sump is that portion of the crankcase at its lower end which is adapted to act as the oil reservoir, the detachable cover at the bottom usually receives this title. A glance at Fig. 11 will show that the oil level is much higher than the joint face to which the cover is attached, so that the sump does in fact comprise the cover and the lower part of the crankcase.

The bottom cover—or sump as we shall call it—has appeared in two forms. On the original Model S7 engine it was quite shallow, and the filter tray which fitted between it and the bottom crankcase face formed the lower part of the box-like filter which projected upwards into the crankcase, although it was well submerged within the oil supply. With this early sump the total oil capacity was a nominal 3 pints.

When Model S8 was introduced, followed shortly afterwards by the Model S7 de luxe, a deeper sump was fitted which gave a total capacity of about 4 pints, although the makers' instructional literature only claims $3\frac{1}{2}$ pints. With the deeper sump a modified filter tray was adopted, the box filter of which projected downwards into the sump, thus enabling the pump to draw cooler oil from the lowest level.

The introduction of the deeper sump was a great improvement, for it resulted in a lower running temperature for the oil, with a corresponding reduction in the overall engine temperature, higher efficiency and a somewhat greater tolerance towards inferior fuels.

Owners of the early Sunbeam Twins with the shallow sump may fit the deeper model if they wish, and they will find the slight expense and effort will be worth while. The only point calling for a little patience and skill is the fact that the fixing studs are somewhat longer, and the original studs have to be extracted. A new suction pipe has to be fitted to the pump, together with a new filter tray. The makers' part numbers for the new components involved are:

New Sump	.	.	.	.	. 89-198
Filter tray	.	.	.	.	. 89-194
Suction pipe	.	.	.	.	. 89-69
Sump studs	.	.	.	.	. 89-68

Clutch

This is of the dry-plate type, for which lubrication is neither required nor desirable. To function properly it must remain absolutely dry, and in no circumstances must oil of any kind be allowed to come into contact with it.

Gearbox

This is self-contained as regards lubrication, and a supply of oil is carried in the lower part of the box, lubrication being by splash. The correct quantity of oil is 2 pints, and this is controlled for filling and topping up by a level plug at the side which is removed, together with the filler plug at the top when this operation is carried out. To fill to the correct level, pour the oil in through the filling orifice until it starts running out at the level-plug hole. Then replace both plugs. Engine oil is suitable for the gearbox.

The Final Drive

The final worm drive has undergone one or two minor alterations since its original introduction, but the lubrication instructions have not been materially altered, except for one item with which we shall deal presently.

Like the gearbox, the worm-drive lubrication is self-contained, and comprises a filler plate at the top and a level plug at the side, enabling the correct amount of lubricant to be poured in when they are both removed.

On present-day Sunbeams there is a drain plug at the bottom of the worm housing, but this item was absent from a few of the earliest models.

The main difference between early Sunbeams and those produced during the last few years, in so far as worm drive lubrication is concerned, is that engine oil was recommended originally, whereas a considerably heavier lubricant of viscosity SAE140 is now required. Actually, this thicker oil is equally suitable for the earlier machines, and owners will find that they will run all the better for it.

Suspension System

The hydraulically damped telescopic front forks now fitted to all Sunbeams require no separate lubrication, since this is provided automatically by the oil used in the hydraulic system. On earlier machines equipped with wick lubrication the most suitable grade of oil was that recommended for the engine.

As regards rear suspension, this calls for no attention, apart from regular grease-gun application once a week. In the case of early models with wick lubrication the correct oil was as for the engine.

Oil Capacities

Engine sump	.	.	.	.	$3\frac{1}{2}$ pints
Gearbox	.	.	.	.	2 pints
Worm drive	.	.	.	.	$\frac{1}{2}$ pint
Front forks	.	.	.	.	$\frac{3}{8}$ pint per leg

Oil and Grease Recommendations

In the makers' Instruction Manual the products of six reputable oil firms are recommended as being suitable for Sunbeam motor cycles and, although there are numerous other brands of oil which are beyond reproach and entirely suitable for Sunbeams, the owner is advised to adhere to the recommended list, because the oils listed have all been thoroughly tested. These remarks apply principally to Home Market owners, but the recommended products may not be universally obtainable overseas. In such cases the best available oil should be used, but the correct viscosity is of prime importance. If too thin an oil is used in hot climates much of it will burn away, and heavy consumption will result. If a thick oil is used in very cold weather, starting will be difficult, and the engine will suffer rapid wear, if not actual seizure, due to sluggish circulation of the thick lubricant.

In the following table, which is reproduced from the makers' Instruction Manual, will be found a complete list of recommended oils and greases, and also a note on overseas conditions.

RECOMMENDED LUBRICANTS

Brand.	Oil.				Grease.
	Summer.	Winter.	Hydraulic front forks only.	Worm drive only.	
Shell .	X100–50	X100–30	X100–20	Dentax 140	Retinax A or C D
Essolube .	50	30	20	Gear oil (heavy)	Esso Grease
B.P. Energol .	SAE50	SAE30	SAE20	SAE140	Energrease C3
Castrol .	Grand Prix	XL	Castrolite	D	Castrolease (heavy)
Mobiloil .	D	A	Arctic	Mobilube C	Mobil-Grease No. 2

FOR THE OVERSEAS MARKET.—Recommendations as above if these are obtainable. If not, the following rule

should be observed: The higher the temperature the
higher is the SAE Number required.

For summer	.	.	.	. SAE50
For winter	.	.	.	. SAE30–SAE20
Front forks	.	.	.	. SAE20
Rear drive	.	.	.	. SAE140

CHAPTER VII

MAINTENANCE

OWING to its modern design involving unit construction with shaft-drive final transmission, the maintenance required on the Sunbeam Twin is reduced to an absolute minimum. It is nevertheless essential to follow a regular routine of examination in order to check and rectify if necessary any adjustable points at which wear is liable to occur and, of course, to provide correct lubrication whenever this is required.

In the following notes the various items requiring adjustment or lubrication, or both, are dealt with individually, and the resulting analysis of the machine's maintenance requirements is then summarised in tabular form for greater convenience of reference.

ENGINE

Valve Clearance

Often called tappet clearance (although this is incorrect in the case of the Sunbeam, as it has no tappets), this refers to the essential amount of play in the valve-operating system. It is essential in order to ensure that, under all conditions, the valve is firmly on its seat when in the closed position. Owing to the varying temperature in an engine, not only from time to time, but also from part to part, it may almost be said that the valve clearance is never the same from one minute to another. This does not matter very much: the really important thing is that under the worst possible conditions there must still be *some* clear-

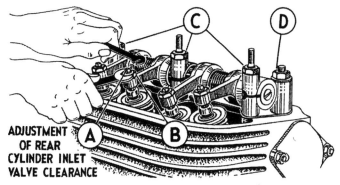

FIG. 12.—ADJUSTMENT OF REAR-CYLINDER INLET-VALVE
CLEARANCE.

A. Pin.
B. Lock-nut.
C. Rocker shaft holding nuts.
D. Cylinder-head nut.

ance. At the same time there should not be too much. Under extreme conditions insufficient clearance may result in the valves being held off their seats, in which case engine power will suffer and the valves themselves will become burnt. Too much clearance will only result in excessive mechanical noise, without any benefit in other directions.

The recommended valve clearance for the Sunbeam is 0·018 in. *with the engine cold*. Note the words in italics. The operation is easily carried out when the cylinder-head cover is removed by taking off the three nuts.

Place the machine on its stand and turn the engine by means of the kick-starter. This latter operation will be found easier if the sparking-plugs are first removed. It is, of course, essential that any valve whose clearance is being checked or adjusted should be closed, and its rocker on the base circle or neutral portion of the cam. To obtain this position for the front-cylinder inlet valve turn the engine until the rear-cylinder inlet valve is fully open. (These valves are the second and third respectively from the front.) Similarly, to set the rear inlet valve in the correct position, turn the engine until the front inlet valve is fully open. Follow the same procedure exactly for the two exhaust valves, the front-cylinder exhaust valve being number one from the front and the rear number four.

Having turned the engine until the valve under consideration is in its correct position, insert the 0·018-in. feeler gauge supplied in the tool-kit between the valve stem and rocker. If the adjustment is correct this should slide in easily, but without play.

To adjust the clearance, if it is found to be incorrect, hold the pin (A, Fig. 12) and release the lock-nut B (suitable spanners are provided in the tool-kit). Then, holding nut B, screw pin A up or down as required until the correct amount of play is obtained. When this is done, hold A with its spanner and tighten nut B very securely. When B is properly tightened, check the play again, to make certain that it has not been altered while tightening the nut. Check and adjust all four adjusters in the same manner, and do not forget that this must be done while the engine is quite cold. Finally, replace the cylinder-head cover and the sparking-plugs.

Camshaft Driving Chain

On engines produced until the middle of the 1951 Season the tensioner for the camshaft chain was of the simple Weller type, and non-adjustable. This was quite satisfactory in general, but a few cases of persistent fracture of the spring blade led the manufacturers to substitute a greatly superior tensioner of their own design, comprising a spring-loaded pivoted steel slipper with a hard-chrome bearing face. All engines fitted with earlier tensioners can now be converted to the new type, but this work is really beyond the scope of the average owner, and it should be entrusted to a Sunbeam dealer or the Factory Service Department. There are two conversion kits, one for the original S7 engines, and the other for the S8 series fitted to Models S7 de luxe and S8, and commencing with Engine No. S8-104.

Adjustment of the new tensioner, which is illustrated in Fig. 3a, is carried out in the following manner. With the engine cold turn it until an exhaust valve begins to open, thus slackening the chain on the tensioner side.

Remove cover held by two screws, A (Fig. 3a), slacken pinch bolt B. This will allow the tensioner to bear correctly on the slack run of the chain. Re-tighten pinch bolt and replace cover, together with its fibre washer and the fibre washer for each retaining screw.

Clutch Adjustment

In order that the clutch may transmit the full engine power without slipping, it is essential that the plates should be held firmly together by the full pressure of the springs. The position here is analogous to that described for the correct seating of the valves in the sense that this can be ensured only if there is a certain amount of clearance in the operating mechanism, which in the case of the clutch comprises the handlebar lever, the bowden cable, the actuating lever on the gearbox and the push-rod which slides in the hollow gearbox mainshaft. This play can easily be felt at the handlebar lever, and should amount to not less than $\frac{1}{8}$ in. of motion at the end of the lever, which represents about $\frac{1}{16}$ in. at the cable.

As the clutch friction surfaces wear, this play becomes less, and it should be checked, and rectified if necessary, at intervals of not more than a thousand miles. Adjustment is easily carried out at the cable stop on the gearbox lug at the left-hand side. Release the lock-nut and screw the adjuster in to increase the play, and out to reduce it. The range of adjustment provided by this arrangement is sufficient for very many thousands of miles, and in most cases it is adequate for the entire life of the machine. The rate of clutch wear is extremely slow and usually negligible, but careless handling and persistent and unnecessary slipping during engagement will actuate the process. The habit of driving on the clutch once so prevalent amongst motor cyclists, but now happily almost a thing of the past, was responsible for much of the rapid wear and overheating of the clutches, and the Sunbeam version, sturdy and of ample margin though it is, is just as liable as any other clutch to suffer from this form of abuse, which, considering the flexible nature of the engine and the ample flywheel, is totally unnecessary.

On some of the earlier models provision was made for restoring vanished play by reversing the actuating lever, which was cranked for this purpose, but experience over a period convinced the makers that this experiment was superfluous, and it was therefore discontinued.

Apart from a periodical check of the control adjustment, the clutch requires no attention, although some riders favour the practice of applying a few drops of oil occasionally, or a touch of grease to the point where the actuating lever operates the push-rod.

Steering-head

This is one of the most important bearings in a motor cycle, and yet it is the one which very often gets the least attention. Correct adjustment of the steering-head bearings is essential for maximum road holding and

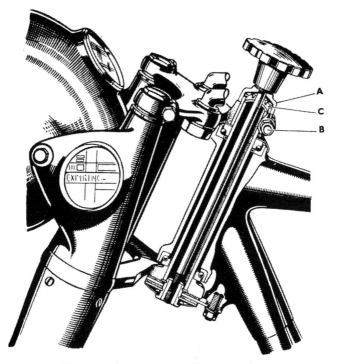

FIG. 13.—ADJUSTMENT OF STEERING-HEAD.
A. Lock nut.   B. Pinch bolt.   C. Adjusting sleeve.

stability, both of which will be impaired if the bearings are run too slack or too tight, not to mention the rapid rate of wear which is liable to ensue. So check the steering-head every thousand miles.

It is very difficult to test for adjustment when the front wheel is on the ground. The front of the machine should therefore be lifted high enough to enable a suitable box or block of wood to be placed under the sump, so that the front wheel is free. Then test the steering-head for

F

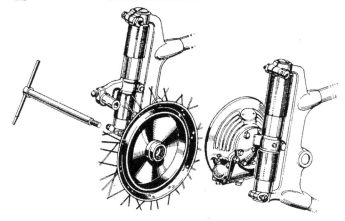

FIG. 14.—REAR WHEEL AS FITTED TO MODELS S7 AND S7 DE LUXE, SHOWING QUICK DETACHING ARRANGEMENT.

play by standing in front of the machine and taking hold of the fork legs, one in each hand. Holding the forks thus, try to rock them up and down, having first slackened the steering-damper right off.

There should be no perceptible play, and yet the forks should rotate freely when the handlebar is turned. If incorrect, adjust in the following manner:

Unscrew the steering-damper knob with stem, and then the steering-head lock-nut A (Fig. 13). Slacken the pinch bolt B and tighten the adjusting sleeve C until any slackness has been taken up. Do not over-tighten, or steering will be stiff and the ball races may be damaged. Tighten the pinch bolt after adjustment is complete, and then replace the steering-head lock-nut and damper knob. It is advisable to re-check the adjustment after tightening the lock-nut.

In the case of the original Model S7 (i.e., up to and including Frame No. S7–2205) the steering-head adjustment was carried out in a somewhat simpler manner.

Having released the pinch-bolts and the steering-damper as described above, it was only necessary to screw the hexagon immediately under the steering-damper knob up or down, as the case might be, in order to obtain correct adjustment, thereafter re-tightening the pinch-bolts and re-setting the steering-damper pressure.

Apart from this periodical examination of the steering-head adjustment, the only maintenance required is a little weekly attention to ensure adequate lubrication.

Wheels and Hubs

The wheels fitted to Model S7 and S7 de luxe are quickly detachable and interchangeable. In fact, with the knock-out type of spindle fitted they are often described

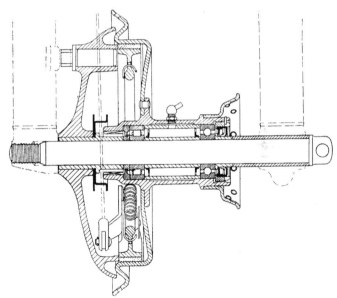

FIG. 15.—SECTION OF QUICKLY DETACHABLE AND INTER-CHANGEABLE WHEEL (SHOWN IN S7 FRONT FORKS).

as instantly detachable, for the simple unscrewing of the spindle from one end, having first released a simple pinch-bolt, enables the wheel to drop out, leaving the brake undisturbed (see Figs. 14 and 15).

As distinct from this, the front wheel of Model S8 is quickly detachable in the sense that its spindle is of the knock-out variety, but before removing the wheel it is necessary to disconnect the front brake control, as the brake, being part of the wheel, comes away with it (Fig. 16).

Apart from these differences, all Sunbeam wheels are really quickly detachable, and they have the further advantage of requiring no hub adjustment, since the bearings are all of the journal variety. The S7 type are

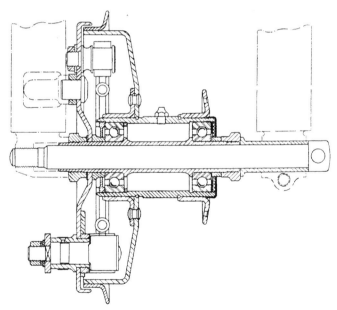

FIG. 16.—SECTION OF MODEL S8 FRONT HUB.

fitted with one ball and one roller bearing, while the front
wheel on Model S8 has two ball bearings.   These bearings
are more than adequate for the loads they have to carry,
and provided that the hubs are regularly lubricated by
grease-gun, they give faultless service throughout the life
of the machine.

When the hubs are originally assembled at the factory
they are packed with grease, and it is therefore only
necessary to " top-up ", as it were, once every thousand
miles by giving two or three strokes of the grease-gun.
Excessive application of the gun will only cause the grease
to ooze out at undesirable places, and some may even find
its way into the brake drum, where its presence would have
a disastrous effect on the efficiency of the brakes, reducing
their stopping power to *nil*.   On no account must oil be
used for hubs.

Brakes

On Model S7 brakes and the rear brake on Model S8 a
simple type of adjustment is provided.   This takes the
form of an adjustable fulcrum for the shoes, the operation
at the lever end, which in any case is enclosed within the
front brake, being left undisturbed.

Apply a spanner to the square head on the adjuster as
shown in Fig. 17, and turn in a clockwise direction.   Note
that the adjuster turns in a series of " clicks ", each
representing a quarter of a turn.   For correct adjustment
turn until you can go no farther, and then slacken back
one click.   This will give a setting for maximum efficiency
with the shoes just clear of the drum when the brake is
off, and close enough for immediate contact when the
brake is applied.

In the case of Model S8 front brake the adjustment
is carried out in the more usual manner, for a knurled
lock-nut and adjuster for the operating cable are mounted

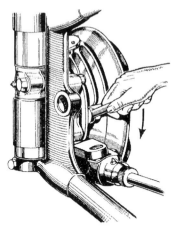

FIG. 17.—METHOD OF BRAKE
ADJUSTMENT.

Spanner should be fitted on the
adjuster and turned in a clockwise
direction as indicated by the arrow.

on a stop lug at the lower end of the offside fork leg. To adjust, release the locknut and screw the adjuster up or down until the correct amount of play is obtained.

The question of the correct amount of play is most important. In the case of the S7 and S8 rear brakes the owner is largely relieved of responsibility in this direction, for the difference between one *click* and the next on the adjuster is sufficient for this purpose. With the cable type of adjuster on S8 it is a different matter, however, and the owner must be careful to see that when the brake is off and the adjustment correct there is still a small amount of lost or free movement of the handlebar lever before the shoes grip when the brake is applied. Such lost motion should be of the order of $\frac{3}{4}$ in. measured at the tip of the lever.

It will be obvious from the above notes that accurate brake adjustment is a matter of great importance, and also that the operation can be carried out satisfactorily only when the wheel is lifted clear of the ground.

As far as lubrication is concerned, none is required except for the rear cam spindle, which, being long and overhung, requires a light touch of the grease-gun once a week.

Engine Suspension

The Sunbeam Twin is probably unique amongst motor cycles in being provided with fully floating power. The engine is, in fact, suspended on rubber, and has a range of free lateral movement which compares easily with the latest and best in modern car practice. It also has a most unusual and highly efficient feature in the shape of a high-frequency vibrated damper, which effectively suppresses the " pins-and-needles " effect that is so troublesome at certain speeds on some power units.

A glance at Fig. 2 will give a clear idea of the engine mounting. There is no metallic contact between the engine and the frame. Connecting the two front down tubes about half-way down from the head-lug is a bracket, and there is a similar bracket between the same pair of tubes under the gearbox where they run horizontally towards the rear, and are often called—illogically enough—the chainstays. Mounted at the centre of these brackets is a large circular block of rubber, and the support lugs on the power unit, one attached to the front of the cylinder block and the other under the gearbox shell, rest on these rubber blocks. These are the only supports for the power unit within the frame.

A line drawn through the two supports passes diagonally through the engine and actually intersects its centre of gravity. Another line more or less at right angles to this, and also passing through the centre of gravity, is determined by the positions of the two pairs of snubbers, one near the dynamo at the lower front and the other under the saddle-peak support lug. These snubbers are simply rubber buffers adjustable for lateral position, and so set that quite an appreciable amount of engine movement is permissible before they touch.

Built in with the upper pair of snubbers is the high-

frequency damper. This consists of two steel plates, one
fixed to the engine and the other to the frame, with a fabric
friction plate between them, the three being held in contact
by an enclosed spring. The latter is free-set and non-
adjustable, so that the act of tightening its bolt automatically provides the correct pressure for efficient damping of the high-frequency vibration.

Adjustment of Snubbers

For maximum efficiency it is essential that the snubbers
should be in correct adjustment, and they should be
checked and adjusted if necessary every 1000 miles. The
bottom pair of snubbers are situated one on each side of
the front frame member, and they operate against fibre
stops mounted in the crankcase and held by screws. The
clearance between each snubber and its stop is 0·015–
0·020 in. when the engine is in its central static position.
To adjust a snubber, release its lock-nut, and then
screw it bodily in or out as the case may be until the
correct clearance is obtained. Then tighten the lock-
nut.

In the case of the top snubbers situated just above
the distributor at the rear of the cylinder-head cover, the
clearance should also be 0·015–0·020 in. They are
attached to brackets on the engine high-frequency damper
plate, and operate against a metal tongue bolted to the
clip-lug on the top-frame tube. They are adjusted by
fitting shims between them and their brackets.

Instructions regarding the setting of the engine-suspen-
sion system from first principles (i.e., finding the correct
setting when all the parts have been dismantled, and the
engine is being re-fitted to the frame after an overhaul)
are given on pages 92 and 114, together with an exploded
view of the combined top snubbers and high-frequency
damper.

MAINTENANCE TABLE

Adjustments

The following items should be checked and adjusted if necessary at the mileage intervals stated.

Item.						Mileage.
Valve clearance	.	.	.	.	.	2000
Camshaft chain	.	.	.	.	.	2000
Clutch control .	.	.	.	.	.	1000
Steering-head .	.	.	.	.	.	1000
Brakes .	.	.	.	.	.	1000
Engine mounting	.	.	.	.	.	1000

Lubrication (Oil)

Item.				Mileage.	Capacity.
Engine sump	.	.	.	2000	$3\frac{1}{2}$ pints
Gearbox .	.	.	.	2000	2 pints
Rear drive .	.	.	.	2000	$\frac{1}{2}$ pint
Front forks	.	.	.	Top up periodically as required	$\frac{3}{8}$ pint per leg

Lubrication (Grease Gun)

The following items should be greased weekly :

Steering-head	Rear suspension
Brake cross-shaft	Rear universal joint
Saddle front pivot (S7)	Central stand
Brake pedal	

Other Items

Hubs . . . every 1000 miles

Rear-brake cam spindle . . . weekly but only a very small quantity

Saddle suspension (S7) . . . remove and pack with grease annually.

General

The above paragraphs complete the Sunbeam maintenance requirements, apart from various items which call for regular lubrication by grease-gun or oil-can. These are given in the preceding table, which also includes recommendations with regard to the draining and refilling of the engine sump, gearbox and rear drive.

CHAPTER VIII

DISMANTLING, RECTIFICATION AND REASSEMBLY

Removing Unit from Frame

PRELIMINARY work before an attempt is made to remove the unit includes dismantling of exhaust system and carburetter, distributor and dynamo. For the latter see Fig. 18, which gives an exploded view showing the method of attachment of the end plate and yoke to the crankcase, and the armature to the end of the crankshaft. Note that the central securing bolt has a left-hand thread.

Drain the sump and gearbox by removing the drain plugs under each unit, and the respective filling caps. This operation is carried out more easily when the oil is warm—immediately after a run. When empty, replace the plugs lightly for safety's sake, taking care not to mislay the fibre washers.

Remove the petrol pipe and drain tank, and then take the tank off, noting that it is insulated from the top tube by two rubber cushions. Disconnect the speedometer drive on top of the gearbox, then remove the battery, the control box and battery container. It is not necessary to disconnect the lighting harness, as this is long enough to allow the boxes to be placed on top of the saddle, but the distributor cover must be unclipped.

Next disconnect the clutch cable at the gearbox end and the two bolts A (Fig. 19) on the universal joint at front end of shaft. Note for reassembly that the bushes for the universal joint bolts are spigoted in pairs on alternate sides,

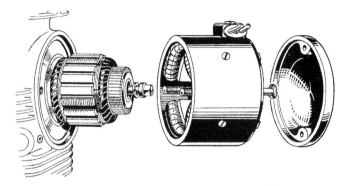

FIG. 18.—EXPLODED VIEW OF DYNAMO SHOWING METHOD OF
ATTACHMENT OF END PLATE AND YOKE TO CRANKCASE.

and also that the forks at each end of the shaft must be in line.

It is also necessary to remove the engine-damper plate D (Fig. 20). First remove the nut M, this will release the spring pressure unit on the damper plate. Then remove the two attachment bolts E by unscrewing their respective nuts when the damper plate, together with its four reinforced plates C and the friction disc F, will come away. Remove the lower frame-clip nut and its bolt B to release the tongue A, and slacken off the upper frame-clip nut so that the frame-clip bracket O can be slid along the top tube out of the way.

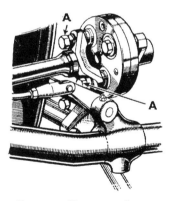

FIG. 19.—UNIVERSAL JOINT.
Clutch cable should be detached at the gearbox end and at the two bolts, A.

When the above items have been disconnected, the

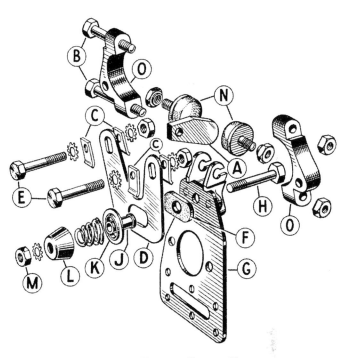

FIG. 20.—EXPLODED VIEW OF ENGINE HIGH-FREQUENCY DAMPER.

A. Tongue.
B. Retaining bolt.
C. Plates.
D. Damper plates.
E. Bolts for reinforcement plates.
F. Friction disc.
G. Snubber plate.

H. Bolt.
J. Distance piece.
K. Spring.
L. Cap.
M. Cap nut.
N. Torque reaction snubber.
O. Frame-clip bracket.

FIG. 21.—REMOVAL OF GEAR-
BOX COVER.

The gearbox side-cover plate is held in position by eight screws. These should be taken out and the gearbox cover can then be removed, together with the kick-starter and foot gear-change mechanism.

(B.S.A. Motor Cycles Ltd.)

actual process of engine dismounting can be undertaken. The power unit is mounted on two rubber cushions, one at the rear of gearbox and the other at a point level with the cylinder-head joint face above the dynamo.   Before these are removed, place a block of wood of suitable height under the sump to take the weight of the unit.   Then take off the nuts and bolts and lift the engine complete out of the frame, withdrawing it from the offside.

Note.—It is not necessary to remove the frame front cross member.

Removing Gearbox

This is attached to the crankcase by five studs, and the gearbox is easily taken off when the nuts are removed. Note that the front end of the gearbox mainshaft is splined for coupling to the clutch centre, and that the clutch remains in position on the engine crankshaft when the gearbox is withdrawn.

Dismantling Gearbox

First take off the kick-starter and foot gear-change pedals. These are held by pinch bolts engaging in grooves in their shafts, their radial position being located by splines.   Withdraw the pinch bolts completely.   Then undo the eight large cheese-head screws holding the gearbox side-cover plate in position on the nearside, and then take off the cover, which will come away with the kickstarter and foot gear-change mechanism as seen in Fig. 21. Then remove the gear indicator.

Remove the universal joint coupling and its flange from the rear end of the layshaft by withdrawing the split pin and then unscrewing the central nut.   Then withdraw the clutch push-rod from the centre of the gearbox mainshaft from the front end of the gearbox, and take off the

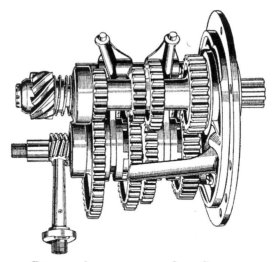

FIG. 22.—ARRANGEMENT OF GEAR CLUSTER.
When dismantling the relative position of the parts should be studied with a view to subsequent reassembly.

circlip which locates the mainshaft kick-starter ratchet on the splines at the rear end of the mainshaft.

The gearbox front-bearing housing, which is attached to the gearbox shaft inside the clutch-bell housing, is held by eight studs and nuts, which are locked in pairs by special tab washers. Release the latter before the nuts are unscrewed, and when the nuts are off, the bearing housing can be drawn out. This can be followed by the gearbox mainshaft, layshaft and selector shaft complete with their gears, which should come out in a single cluster.

When the gear cluster is removed from the gearbox and laid out on a bench it is easily dismantled, and no special instructions are necessary with regard to this, except the usual note that the relative positions of the parts be studied with a view to subsequent reassembly (Fig. 22).

Dismantling Foot Gear-change

This mechanism comprises five main components, which are the shaft A (Fig. 23) with operating arm B, the cam-actuating plate C, the pawl plate D and the cam-and-ratchet plate E. In operation, movement of the gear-change pedal causes arm B to describe an arc, and this in turn rocks the cam-actuating plate C, which is coupled to it through the medium of a peg and a slot seen in the illustration. The cam-actuating plate is coupled to the pawl plate also through the intermediary of a slot and peg, and as it swings on a larger radius than the distance between the centre of rotation of the pawl plate and the peg on the latter, its fulcrum being at F, there is a multiplying action by virtue of which the angle of movement of the pawl plate for one stroke of the pedal is greater than the angular movement of the latter. The pawl plate carries two pawls G, which are spring-loaded and which engage with ratchet teeth H on the cam plate. For every stroke of the gear-change pedal therefore, the pawl plate moves the cam plate one tooth, and as the pedal returns to its normal position, so does the pawl plate, leaving the cam plate in the new position to which it has been moved. As there are three right-hand ratchet teeth and three left-hand ratchet teeth on the cam plate, this component is enabled to move three successive stages in either direction, and as it does so, the cam grooves J on its other face operate the gear-selector forks, causing them to move fore and aft along their shaft for selection of the appropriate gears. Location of the gears when engaged is provided by a spring-loaded plunger operating in notches machined in the periphery of the cam plate.

Coupled to the cam plate by a peg is a short rod connected to a lever attached to a sleeve mounted on the pedal shaft A, and at the pedal end of the shaft and

FIG. 23.—EXPLODED VIEW OF
GEAR-CHANGE UNIT.

A. Shaft.
B. Operating arm.
C. Cam-actuating plate.
D. Pawl plate.
E. Cam-and-ratchet plate.
F. Fulcrum of swing of cam-
   actuating plate.
G. Pawls.
H. Ratchet teeth.
J. Cam grooves.

(B.S.A. Motor Cycles Ltd).

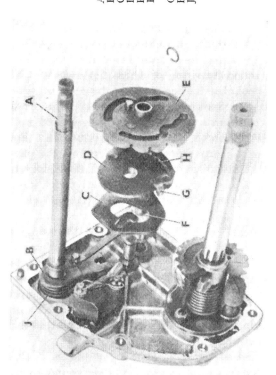

[*B.S.A. Motor Cycles Ltd.*

FIG. 24.—EXPLODED VIEW OF CLUTCH MECHANISM.

keyed to it is a short indicator sleeve, which terminates in a flange outside the gearbox shell. This is marked I N 2 3 4, the particular figure or letter adjacent to an arrow on the gearbox shell indicating which gear is in engagement.

If the foot gear-change mechanism is dismantled for any reason, make certain on reassembly that the pawl spring H is correctly engaged with the pawls, as illustrated, and also that the large hairpin spring J, which serves as a double-acting return spring for the pedal, is also correctly engaged with the operating arm.

Removing Clutch

This cannot be removed as a complete assembly. Fig. 24 shows an exploded view of the clutch, which should enable dismantling and reassembly to be carried out without difficulty. The nuts on the six driving pegs (A) should be removed, noting that the clutch-spring pressure is released as this is done. A certain amount of

FIG. 25.—METHOD OF RELEASING CRANKSHAFT NUT AT THE FLYWHEEL.

The crankshaft can sometimes be released by hand pressure using a box or tubular spanner. If the nut is very tight a hammer must be applied to the spanner.

(B.S.A. Motor Cycles Ltd).

care should therefore be exercised as the nuts are finally unscrewed. The outer driving plate B, followed by the clutch centre, or driven plate C, and then the inner or spring pressure plate, can be withdrawn, and the springs should be taken off and placed on one side, leaving the flywheel in position. When the plates are removed, the mainshaft nut holding the flywheel will be exposed, and this must be unscrewed for removal of the latter, which also functions as the clutch body. This nut, which has a right-hand thread, is very tight, and is locked by means of a tab-washer, which must be released before removal. To unscrew the nut, use a suitable box or tubular spanner which provides sufficient leverage and can be operated by hand pressure alone. If not, it may be necessary to release the nut by the use of a hammer applied to the spanner, in which case the inertia of the flywheel is sufficient to absorb the shock and prevent the whole assembly from turning (see Fig. 25). If the nut is released by hand pressure alone it will be necessary to hold the flywheel by means of a suitable lever.

When the nut is removed the flywheel can be withdrawn from the shaft, although it will be necessary to exert considerable pressure in order to release it from its taper. A suitable extractor tool of the " pulley-drawer " variety may be used for this purpose (see Fig. 25a), or it may be found possible to release the flywheel by giving the face of the flywheel rim a few sharp blows with a copper or rawhide mallet. Remove the key and place it on one side.

Big-end Bearings

It is possible to dismantle these when the engine is still in the frame, but the operation is much more conveniently performed when the engine is removed, particularly if it is desired to withdraw the pistons and connecting-rods.

FIG. 25(a).—REMOVAL OF FLYWHEEL.

The sump is held in position by twelve studs and nuts, four of the former being visible in Fig. 26, and when the nuts are removed it may be taken off together with the filter tray.   If the joint washers do not come away with the sump they should be carefully detached and, if in sound condition, put on one side for replacement when reassembling.

When the filter tray is removed the big-ends are exposed, and these should be brought to the lowest position by turning the engine to bottom dead centre.   The big-end caps can now be taken off in the normal manner. Note the provision of split pins for the big-end bolts, and make a note also of the tightness of the nuts as an indication as to how tight they must be made on reassembly.

The actual big-end bearings are special white-metal liners, and these are supplied ready for immediate fitment to the connecting-rods.   Replacement, in the rare event of this becoming necessary, is therefore simple, as no fitting or scraping is needed.   Note that in accordance with normal practice the big-end caps and rods are similarly marked on one of the bolt bosses in order that they may be correctly put together.   Note also that this marking occurs on the side of the rod nearest to the sump oil orifice (i.e., on the nearside of the engine).   This is important.   If the crankpin journals or the main rear journal are worn oval more than a few thousandths of an inch, it may be necessary to have them re-ground, and this will call for special big-end liners or main bearing as the case may be.   These may be obtained on application to the Sunbeam Service Department or to the local dealer. For these reasons replacements should be of extremely rare occurrence, and are not likely to be required until very considerable mileages have been covered.

With the removal of the big-end caps, the pistons and

FIG. 26.—WITHDRAWAL OF CRANKSHAFT.

rods are ready for withdrawal from the cylinder block. These are taken out from the top. A word of warning is necessary here: the overall width of the connecting-rod big-end is only slightly less than the cylinder bore, and the bolts themselves are specially machined on the heads for clearances. See therefore that the bolts, which are, of course, loose by now, are turned to the correct position before attempting to slide the rod into the cylinder bore. Otherwise there is a risk of jamming and scoring the bore.

Pistons

The gudgeon pins, which are fully floating, are located by means of circlips, and these are easily removed with the aid of suitable pliers.

When cold the gudgeon pins may be rather tight in the piston bosses, although they are, of course, perfectly free when the engine has warmed up to its normal running temperature. It may therefore be necessary to drive them out of the pistons by the application of a hammer to a suitable punch, carefully supporting the piston meanwhile in order to avoid distortion. Preferably, the gudgeon pin can be released by warming the piston for a few seconds by wrapping it in a rag which has been soaked in warm water.

If the pistons giving a compression ratio of 6·8 or 7·2 to 1 are fitted, they are not reversible, due to their specially shaped heads. It is advisable therefore to mark each piston inside the skirt in order to ensure its replacement in the correct position, and, of course, in its own cylinder bore.

The main object in removing the pistons, apart from any special circumstances calling for the complete dismantling of the engine, is to examine the skirts and rings, for size and condition. Excessive piston tap, heavy oil

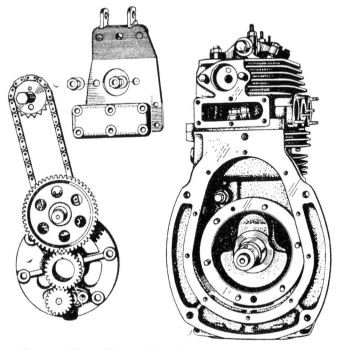

Fig. 27.—Valve Timing Gear Showing Correct Position.

consumption and a general deterioration in engine performance may be due in part, at least, to worn pistons, bores and rings.

The best way to examine the piston-rings for wear is to place them in the bores, after removal from the pistons, and measure the gaps with feelers. These should be not less than 0·004 in., and not more than 0·020 in.

Apart from wear, the rings should also be examined for condition of bearing surfaces. If these are scored or discoloured, the rings should be replaced. If the rings seem to have lost some of their " springiness " or if their free gap does not appear sufficient, both of which items will be immediately apparent to the experienced owner, replacement will be advisable.

Note when replacing the two upper rings that these are tapered slightly. To facilitate assembly they are marked " Top " on their upper faces.

Timing Gear

An exploded view of this is seen in Fig. 27, which makes dismantling and reassembly quite straightforward. Note that when the flywheel is removed, access to the timing gear cannot be gained until the sheet-steel partition carrying the oil seal for the mainshaft is detached. This is held by ten screws, the topmost of which is specially lengthened to act as a trap for the timing chain when the latter is detached from its top sprocket, and thus to prevent its falling down into the lower part of the timing chest and jamming there. After removing the partition, therefore, the top screw should be replaced.

Oil Pump

This is built into the bearing housing, and is shown dismantled in Fig. 28. The cover plate is fixed to the housing by two studs and nuts, the latter being slotted and wired for locking purposes. The driving pinion is a press-fit on its spindle and held by a taper-pin. It should not be removed unless absolutely necessary (see also Fig. 26).

Removing Crankshaft

To remove the crankshaft first detach the dynamo from the front end, removing the parts in the order seen in the exploded view in Fig. 18 (page 92).

The gearbox, clutch and the partition plate holding the

crankshaft oil seal will already have been removed as described above, and so also will the sump, the connecting-rods and pistons, and the timing sprocket and chain. Therefore, it is only necessary now to release the bearing housing by undoing the six nuts on the fixing studs, and the crankshaft can then be drawn out as seen in Fig. 26.

The engine-shaft pinion which drives the timing gear can then be removed by means of an extractor. It is keyed on to the shaft and is a press fit. Alternatively, this pinion can be removed before crankshaft withdrawal, in which case the bearing housing will also be detached from its fixing studs before the crankshaft is disturbed. If the crankshaft is tight in the bearing housing a few taps with a soft mallet or punch will release it. If desired the bearing itself can be driven or pressed out of its

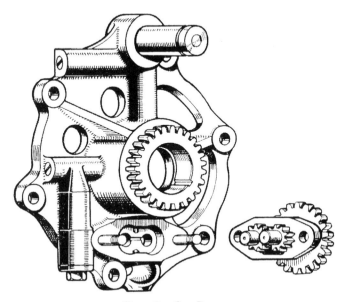

FIG. 28.—OIL PUMP

housing after the crankshaft is removed. This bearing is located in one direction by a circlip fitted to a groove in the housing. On the other side of the circlip (i.e., in front of it) a spring-loaded oil seal is mounted.

Cylinder Liners

The cylinder bores may require rectification eventually, and if wear has taken place two courses of action are open. The bores can be reground up to 0·010 in. oversize, or if the wear is excessive (more than 0·010 in.) new liners should be fitted. As these machines are fitted with detachable liners, these can be removed easily.

Tap out with a mallet and suitable punch from underneath. Note when fitting new liners that the front and rear are different and must be inserted in their correct bores in accordance with the locating dowels fixed in the block.

These remarks do not apply to the original S7, bearing engine numbers up to S7-2371, as the liners were a tight press-fit and could be withdrawn only with special tackle. Liner replacement for these is therefore a job for the repair shop or factory.

Clutch

This is seldom likely to require attention, as it has been designed with an ample margin of transmitting capacity. Prolonged use may, however, result in wear of the friction linings, especially if the machine has been in the hands of an unskilled rider who has formed the habit of slipping his clutch on the least provocation, and this will necessitate the replacement of the fabric rings. This can easily be done by the private individual who is possessed of sufficient skill. Alternatively, the clutch-driven member C (Fig. 24) complete can be returned to the Sunbeam Repair Department or the local dealer for re-lining.

FIG. 29.—FOOT GEAR-
CHANGE MECHANISM IN
NEUTRAL POSITION.

The foot gear-change
mechanism should be
placed in the position
shown, i.e., with the locating plunger in the neutral
notch, before replacing the
gearbox end cover.

(*B.S.A. Motor Cycles Ltd.*)

Should the steel driving plates be badly scored, due to excessive slipping, they should be smoothed off and rubbed down on a surface plate, or replaced if irretrievably damaged.   If the springs show signs of overheating, due possibly to excessive clutch slip, they should be replaced. When new, the free length of these springs is 1·55 in., and if they are much less than this figure it is an indication that they have collapsed and are no longer fit for service.

Reassembling Gearbox

Reassembly of the gearbox calls for a reversal of the process described on page 95.   The end cover will slide home more easily if the kick-starter is depressed once or twice as the cover is moved into position.   Do not forget also to replace the push-rod down the centre of the main-shaft, as this item can easily be overlooked before final assembly.

Before finally replacing the end cover, it should be noted that the pegs on the ends of the gear-selector sliding fork must engage correctly in the cam grooves in the foot gear-change cam plate.   To ensure this, set the gears in neutral, which is between first and second, and turn the foot gear-change mechanism also to the neutral position as indicated by the engagement of the locating plunger in the neutral notch as seen in Fig. 29.   The cover plate should then slide home freely with the gears correctly registered.

Reassembling Engine–Gearbox Unit

Reassembly of the engine is quite straightforward, and calls for no special comment, except that for correct valve timing, when the bearing housing and engine-shaft pinion have been refitted, the latter should be turned until the keyway is vertically upwards as shown in Fig. 27.   The half-time pinion should then be placed on its spindle in such a position that the two teeth marked with a dot engage one on each side of the tooth on the engine-shaft pinion, which is in line with the keyway, and which is also marked with a dot. This position is shown in the illustration. The pinions and sprockets will then be correctly set for the final valve-timing operation.

Valve Timing

Turn the camshaft until the driving-peg hole in the end face of the rear journal is vertically above the camshaft

[B.S.A. Motor Cycles Ltd.

FIG. 30.—COUPLING OF UNITS FOR VALVE AND IGNITION TIMING.

Showing driving-peg hole in the rear journal vertically above the camshaft.

centre, this position being seen in Fig. 30. Next take the camshaft sprocket and engage it in the chain in such a position that the peg is in line with its hole, and then slide it into position. Then replace the bolt and tighten securely. The whole operation will be made a lot easier if the chain tensioner is first released. (For a description of this see page 35.)

Ignition Timing

With the camshaft driving sprocket set as described in the previous paragraph, it will be seen that the peg hole in the sprocket, immediately below the centre, is vacant. This hole is for the driven peg on the distributor coupling flange. Turn this flange until this peg is vertically below the centre (i.e., in line with the hole in the sprocket), when the centres of slots in the external fixing flange are in line with the fixing studs. Then carefully insert the distributor in its housing in the cylinder-head block so that the peg enters the hole in the sprocket. Then lightly tighten up the nuts on the two studs. The distributor coupling flange is permanently pinned to the spindle, so that when the driving peg is engaged as described above the ignition timing will automatically be correct within the range of adjustment provided by the slots on the distributor-body flange. These slots are marked for the best position.

If you have set the distributor in accordance with the marks it will only be necessary finally to tighten the two nuts on the studs, but if you wish for any reason to check the accuracy of the setting, this can be done by turning the engine to top dead centre with the front piston at the firing point (i.e., with both valves closed as ascertained by the feel of the valve-rocker clearance). The distributor rotor arm should then be pointing to the offside and the contact-breaker points should be just opening. The latter item can be checked by rotating the engine slightly in both directions and observing the movement of the points.

Refitting Unit to Frame

For the most part the instructions for removal of the unit are reversed for the refitting process, however, the following important points should be noted:

Having replaced the unit in the frame and bolted up to the two main pre-set rubber mountings (A and B, Fig. 2), refit the tongue (A, Fig. 20) to the frame-clip

H

bracket, locking up the lower retaining bolt B with its nut. Do *not* tighten the upper bolt at this stage. Then *loosely* refit the four reinforcement plates on either side of the damper plate D with two nuts and bolts E, noting that the bevelled edges must be away from the damper plate, as illustrated. Now insert the friction disc F in position and move the damper plate together with the frame-clip bracket forwards until the friction disc is lightly held between the damper plate and the snubber plate G. Replace the bolt H and the distance piece J and position the damper plate D so that the distance piece is located centrally in the hole in the damper plate. Note that the holes in the damper plate are elongated to allow for adjustment (see adjustment of engine-damper snubbers below). Refit the washer and spring K, cap L and nut M, tightening the latter until the cap is locked against the distance piece J.

Adjusting Snubbers

Undo the snubber lock-nut and rotate the snubber until the correct clearance is obtained, finally retightening the lock-nut.

The snubber plate G, Fig. 20, at the top rear of the engine (see also C, Fig. 2) also carries two horizontally opposed torque reaction snubbers N. The clearances between each of these and the central tongue A must be 0·015–0·020 in. with the engine in the static position. Shims may be fitted behind the snubbers to compensate for excessive wear on the rubber faces.

Finally, to ensure that both top and bottom snubbers are synchronised, and that the distance piece through the damper plate D remains in the centre of the elongated slot, the nuts on the bolts E should first be slackened, and the frame-clip bracket O loosened by undoing the nut of the upper bolt B only. Centralise the clip bracket so that

the tongue A is midway between the snubbers N and the
limit of movement (0·030–0·040 in.) in each direction is
simultaneously taken up on both top and bottom snubbers,
i.e., when the upper nearside and the lower offside
snubbers touch simultaneously and vice versa.   This is
accomplished by forcibly tilting the engine in each direction and checking the clearances.

Make sure that the tongue A is locked in the frame-
clip bracket O and then that the nut of the upper bolt B
clamping the clip bracket to the frame top tube and the
two damper-plate retaining nuts of the bolts E are
absolutely tight.

The Rear Drive

The assembly of the worm in its mounting is seen in the
exploded view in Fig. 31.   Reading from right to left the
various parts are, first, the Hardy–Spicer universal joint
fixed to the rear end of the drive shaft from the gearbox ;
second the split-pin and nut by which the coupling flange,
which comes next, is fixed to the worm shaft.   To the
left of this flange is its oil seal, then a bearing housing,
which is attached to the rear-drive casing by four studs
through its flange, next the roller race which runs in the
housing and on which the front end of the worm shaft is
mounted and, finally, on the right-hand side of the casing,
a flinger washer.

Within the casing is the worm shaft with its driving
splines projecting on the right for engagement in the coupling flange.   The worm shaft and the worm are formed in
one solid piece, and the worm can be seen in its normal
position in the casing.

To the left of the casing is a bearing housing for the
special double ball race which comes next, and which
supports the rear end of the worm shaft.   This is followed
by the washer, nut and split pin, which lock the inner race

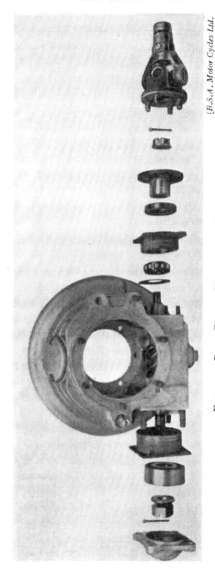

FIG. 31.—REAR DRIVE—WORM-SHAFT ASSEMBLY.

of the double bearing on to the shaft. The last item is the end cap, which is attached to the casing by four studs, and is an extremely important component, as it takes the thrust reaction from the driving effort.

The worm-shaft assembly is virtually self-centring, owing to carefully controlled dimensioning and accurate manufacture. End play is automatically taken up at the rear (i.e., to the left of the illustration) when the nut is tightened on the shaft and the end cap is fixed. The front bearing, being of the roller type is free to float axially, and thus takes up its correct position unaided. When the parts previously described are correctly assembled and the two worm-shaft nuts and the eight stud nuts are properly tightened, the worm should be able to spin freely without shake. The worm shaft can be tested in this manner only when the phosphor-bronze worm wheel and the remainder of the rear-drive unit are absent, as indicated in Fig. 31.

These other items form a second unit within the rear-driving casing, and comprise the worm wheel, its bearings and the means by which its motion is transmitted to the rear wheel. These are shown in Fig. 32. It will be seen that the worm wheel, which is a particularly substantial unit, runs on two ball races, which fit inside it, one on each side with a row of internal teeth between them, these being machined in the internal periphery of the wheel. The ball race on the right is supported on a spigot on the component seen on the extreme right of Fig. 31. This is the rear-drive-housing end cover, which also acts as the offside rear-suspension bracket (see also Fig. 34), and which is machined from a high-tensile aluminium-alloy forging. The left-hand, or inner, ball race is carried on a housing attached to the back face of the rear-drive casing.

The remaining item in Fig. 31 is the one which looks

FIG. 32.—REAR DRIVE—WORM-WHEEL ASSEMBLY.

like a double gear pinion, but which is, in reality, the coupling dog. The larger external toothed portion engages in the internal teeth in the worm wheel, and the smaller toothed portion, when in the assembled position, projects through the central hole in the back face of the rear-drive housing (i.e., on the extreme left) and engages in hollow splines formed in the wheel hub, thus providing the drive to the rear wheel. Two final items not illustrated are first, the rear-wheel spindle, which passes through the hub, through the worm-wheel assembly, and screws into the centre of the spigot on the end cover on the right ; and, second, a distance piece which lies within the hollow coupling dog, and through which the wheel spindle passes. The object of this is to allow the wheel spindle when tightened to lock the assembly solid, while leaving the coupling dog free to float and the worm wheel free to turn on its bearings.

As in the case of the worm-shaft assembly the worm-wheel components are so accurately machined that correct alignment is ensured, but shims are available as a means of holding the worm wheel dead central with respect to the worm below it. This can easily be checked by marking the parts with blue and spinning a few turns. The markings should be central on the flanks of the worm-wheel teeth. A shim is seen on the end-cover spigot.

The part numbers of the shims are as follows :

        89–5635 : 0·002 in. thick
        89–5636 : 0·003 in. thick.

Rear-drive Maintenance

Provided that the unit is regularly lubricated in accordance with the recommendations given elsewhere in this book (see page 89) it will continue to give faultless service for long periods. During operation, however, a slow but inevitable rate of wear occurs at the bronze

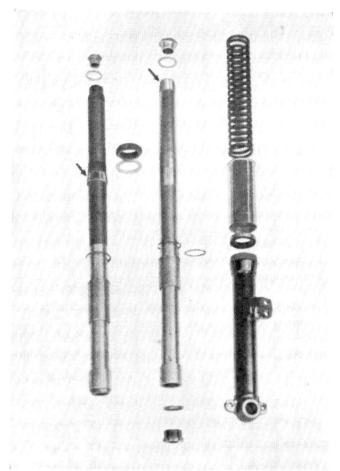

FIG. 33.—EXPLODED VIEW OF FRONT FORKS.

worm wheel, and on removing the drain plug at the bottom of the casing the owner may be surprised to see yellow metallic particles in suspension in the oil. This is no occasion for alarm, and may indeed be considered normal for this type of device.

The presence of this product of wear in the lubricant emphasises the importance of draining and re-filling at regular intervals. If it is decided to swill out the casing after draining and before pouring in fresh oil, do not use paraffin for this purpose, but preferably one of the proprietary flushing oils, or light machine oil of the " hydrocarbon " class.

After very great mileages or after prolonged periods of extra heavy duty, especially if the lubrication has not received proper attention, the wear at the worm wheel teeth may become excessive, as indicated by an abnormal amount of backlash between drive and over-run. Eventually the flanks of the worm wheel teeth may show signs of breaking up and the surfaces may become pitted. When either of these stages is reached it is time to fit new worms and wheels, together with a new pin. The worms and wheels are specially produced in matching pairs, and must not be used separately ; even new parts will not run together satisfactorily unless they are a matched pair, and a new worm wheel with an old worm, or a new worm with an old wheel—although this latter combination is hardly likely to materialise, because the worms seldom wear—will obviously be unsuitable.

Front Forks

These call for very little maintenance indeed, and provided that the oil level in the legs is correctly maintained they will continue to function at maximum efficiency almost indefinitely.

As in the case of all telescopic forks, those fitted to the

[B.S.A. Motor Cycles Ltd.

FIG. 34.—REAR SUSPENSION.

The illustration shows method of dismantling rear suspension. This operation will only be necessary when replacement of the bushes or central column is required. It is also possible that the rear suspension may have to be dismantled following the results of an accident.

Sunbeam Models depend upon mechanical soundness for their correct operation, so that if the shafts are bent or otherwise damaged the forks will be put out of action. This so-called weakness of the telescopic type of fork is sometimes advanced as an adverse criticism of the type because it is pointed out that the older girder forks are able to continue functioning despite a certain amount of damage. The writer feels that this is not a particularly convincing argument, because a pair of forks which are not functioning correctly as spring forks, even though they provide a certain amount of deflection, are probably dangerous to ride, and would probably be safer if locked solid. In any case telescopic forks, and particularly those fitted to the Sunbeam Models, are extremely robust, and an impact sufficient to bend their shafts would probably twist other types out of all recognition, and certainly far beyond the stage at which they could continue to function.

Apart from actual damage to the forks, the question of replacements and worn parts is likely to arise—if it ever does during the lifetime of the machine—only when the bushes in which the shafts slide wear unduly, or if the bearing surfaces on the shafts themselves wear to an unreasonable extent. These working parts are thoroughly lubricated, due to the presence of large quantities of oil in the hydraulic system, and the provision of spring-loaded oil seals prevents both the escape of oil and the ingress of dirt. When excessive wear takes place this is betrayed by a perceptible amount of shake in the fork legs, and by perhaps a slight decline in the sweet and positive action of the system, accompanied in extreme cases by a certain amount of noise.

Replacement of the bushes is quite a simple operation, involving, of course, the dismantling of the forks and the removal of the shafts. Note that the taper on the S7 shaft as seen in the left view, in Fig. 33, engages in the bottom fork yoke, whereas on Model S8, seen in the central view, the taper engages in the top yoke. Otherwise, although dimensionally different, the two types of fork are similar in construction and operation. The lower bush is mounted on the bottom end of the fork shaft, and, being lipped, is locked into position by a nut with a washer screwed into the bottom of the shaft. This is clearly seen in the illustration. The outer periphery provides the bearing surface for the sliding fork leg (bottom right view) as it moves up and down. The fork leg carries the upper bush, which is inserted into its upper end, and is held in position by a circlip. Above this is the oil seal referred to previously. Access can be gained to this upper bush only when the oil seal is removed, and unless a suitable clamp is available for un-screwing the sleeve which holds it into position, it is difficult to do this without using the service tools mentioned on page 133. It is understood, however, that some dealers are willing to provide the loan of these and other service tools to private owners for a nominal fee.

Any play or shake in the fork bushes is more easily tested when the complete leg is removed from the assembly and the spring is withdrawn. The leg should then be pulled down until the two bushes are close together, and if it is then possible to feel an appreciable amount of shake when the leg is rocked sideways it is an indication that the bushes require replacement. In these circumstances it is impossible to give an exact ruling of the amount of permissible play, and the owner should rely on common sense and experience. If he does not trust his own judgment in this matter expert advice should be sought, although it will be obvious that while there must be at least a trace of play, any movement in excess of about $\frac{1}{32}$ in. measured at the extreme end of the fork leg when tested in the above manner should be regarded with suspicion.

Rear Suspension

The remarks made above with regard to the long life of the front suspension bearings apply equally to the rear suspension, provided that adequate and regular grease gun lubrication is applied in accordance with the makers' instruction manual.

Fig. 34 shows clearly the method of dismantling the rear suspension unit, but this operation is rarely necessary except in the case of damage resulting from an accident, although the units are so compact and robust that they are virtually damage-proof, or when replacement of the bushes or of the central column becomes necessary on account of wear.

As in the case of the front suspension bearings, it is not advisable to run with an excessive amount of play, because this tends to be cumulative, and a decision regarding the necessity for replacement should be along the same lines as those discussed in the preceding paragraphs, but service experience indicates that this item seldom calls for attention.

CHAPTER IX

RIDING HINTS

From nearly every point of view the Sunbeam Twin
is in a class by itself, and this certainly applies to its
behaviour on the road, and to the particular driving tech-
nique which the owner rapidly acquires during his early
experience of the machine.

The machine is large in appearance, although this is not
necessarily an adverse characteristic—rather the reverse
in the minds of many owners. This appearance is somewhat deceptive, for in weight the Sunbeam is not greatly
different from a host of other twins of similar capacity.
For example the engine–gear unit, though compact, is
bulky, but a large part of it is in aluminium alloy, which
weighs little more than a third of iron or steel.

The frame is simple and light, but is very strong. On
Model S8 the wheels, forks, guards and so forth are quite
normal and standard.

Steering and Stability

The features of the luxurious Model S7 are the enormous
tyres, the splendid mudguards and the imposing front
forks. These may be considered unnecessary refinements,
but without them the model becomes an S8, and the
world-wide army of S7 devotees is a convincing argument
in favour of these super refinements, despite any adverse
effect, however slight or fanciful, they may have on
its rideability.

The great width of the front forks cannot have any effect,
other than beneficial, on steering and road holding. The

massive tyres, and particularly the front, though it is a shade smaller in section than the rear, are held by some to have a flywheel or gyroscopic effect which tends to offer an appreciable amount of resistance to steering. Some say the effect is most marked when turning to the left, and others say it is more noticeable on right turns. When experts disagree there is often very little to quarrel about, and this is certainly so in the case of Model S7. Having rapidly acquired the " feel " of the machine, which need not take more than a mile or two, the rider is thereafter quite unconscious of the presence of large tyres, except for the feeling of added comfort.

Side Windage

So much for flywheel or gyroscopic effect, both of them often abused and frequently misunderstood terms. Another charge sometimes laid against the generous manner in which Model S7 is shod is that the large tyres and guards offer considerable side windage, and that in cross winds or in gusty weather steering will be affected and in extreme cases the machine will be blown right off the road. This is not so, for the percentage increase in side windage over a normal machine and rider is very small indeed, and careful tests indicate that the effect due to this cause is so small as to be undetectable on the road.

In-line Engine

Turning now to another aspect of the road behaviour of the Sunbeams, we might examine the effect, if any, of in-line engine layout with shaft drive. Although this arrangement is almost unique in the annals of British motor cycling, it has been commonly used in other parts of the world, particularly on the Continent of Europe, with every success, and with little complaint or criticism from users. One has to learn to ride a motor cycle anyway, and the difference between the handling of a chaindriven, crankshaft across the frame, motor cycle of the conventional type, and an in-line type is so slight that it passes unnoticed during the tutelary period. In the hands of an experienced rider, the change from one type to the other is unimportant, and represents no greater hardship than that of changing from one make of machine to another. It is merely a matter of adjusting one's ideas to a different mount.

The writer has been told by a user of both types of machine that the two types were equally good under all conditions, and the racing record of at least one Continental shaft-drive model would seem to confirm this. A final thought for unbelievers is that if a flywheel, or pair of flywheels, in rapid rotation offer a resistance to the steering effort, they will do so whenever they are rotating in a vertical plane. This will therefore apply whether they are rotating in line with the frame or across it.

Engine Performance

And now we come to the performance of the engine, and the best way to use it. The Sunbeam unit develops quite a lot of power, and it does so at high speeds. It is a short-stroke engine; in fact, it is over-square, the bore being greater than the stroke, and as such it likes to rev. To get the highest possible performance out of it, therefore, it must be given its head, and full advantage should be taken of the gearbox. Despite earlier remarks about the machine not being unduly heavy, it nevertheless has a considerable mass, and frequent and intelligent use of the gearbox pays ample dividends in the matter of average speeds.

The gearbox is a particularly simple and robust piece of

mechanism, consisting merely of four pairs of gears in constant mesh, with selector mechanism for engaging one pair at a time to the layshaft, and the frictionless bearings are generous. It is therefore capable of unlimited hard work without protest.

Engine Flexibility

Despite its high-revving propensities, however, the Sunbeam Twin is extremely flexible, due to the special design of its combustion chambers, and its rugged construction and rigidity, which ensure high mechanical efficiency at low speeds. The machine may thus be ridden, if desired, with a profound disregard for its more ambitious performance at the higher speed ranges, and confined to the role of a luxurious potter-bus—as indeed many of them are, either solo or with the sidecar equipment.

Starting and Strangler Control

Owing to the coil ignition and the fairly heavy flywheel, starting is very easy, and the tick-over for an air-cooled engine is phenomenally good. To end these few comments on the handling of the Sunbeam Twin some notes are given below on the correct manipulation of the carburetter strangler control, in connection with starting and on the functioning of the two warning lights in the headlamp.

As already stated, the earlier Sunbeams, which were not fitted with air-cleaners, were provided with a strangler control taking the form of a lever at the back of the carburetter intake bell, while air-cleaner models have a plunger rod directly attached to the carburetter air slide. Apart from the obviously different methods of operating these controls, they are similar in effect and function. To start, turn on the petrol, and flood the carburetter

I

lightly by momentarily depressing the tickler on the float-chamber cap. Close the strangler. To operate the present type depress and turn to engage spring lock; to release, turn the other way. On the older types move the lever fully to the rear. Open the throttle twist-grip about one-tenth of a turn.

Next, switch on the ignition by turning the key on the switch panel under the saddle on the right-hand side of the machine to the right, noting, as you do so, that the red and green lights in the back of the headlamp come on.

Then push the kick-starter down with the foot in a deliberate but not excessively violent manner, and the engine should fire at once. In cold weather with a cold engine, one or two depressions of the kick-starter may be necessary.

If starting from cold, let the engine run for a few seconds before attempting to move off, and open the strangler as soon as possible. This device is intended for starting purposes only, for it delivers an extremely rich mixture to the cylinders—far too rich, in fact, for ordinary running. If it is left in operation for more than a second or two after starting, it will produce harmful results, because either the excess petrol will condense in the cylinders and cause dilution of the lubricating oil, or it will produce a heavy carbon deposit in the combustion chambers and foul the sparking-plugs. At the same time it will result in heavy petrol consumption.

When the engine is warm it is not necessary to use the strangler, even for starting, and the rider should make a point of never using it unless absolutely necessary.

Headlamp Warning Lights

The engine lubrication green warning light in the headlamp goes out as soon as the engine starts, and re-appears only when the oil pressure drops, indicating

that topping-up of the sump is necessary to restore full
working pressure.

It is quite normal for the green light to come on sometimes when the engine is running at a slow tick-over.
The red ignition warning light goes out as soon as the
dynamo begins to charge.

CHAPTER X

SERVICE TOOLS

PRACTICALLY all of the work described in this book can be carried out with ordinary tools such as those found in any well-equipped private garage or workshop.

Many of the operations are, however, greatly facilitated by the use of proper Service Tools and, while it is hardly likely that the average private owner will wish to purchase all or indeed any of them, a complete list is given on the following page, because of its general usefulness, and also because the knowledge that a properly designed Service Tool produced by the makers of the machine is a helpful piece of information for rider and repairer alike, especially if the possibility of arranging for the loan of one exists.

The tools given in the text referred to above are recommended to repairers whose equipment already includes the more usual types of tools which are suitable for general purposes, and who do not therefore have to consider the position from the point of view of original equipment for a new establishment. They are intended rather as a guide to repairers who appreciate the convenience of having tools specially designed for the expeditious handling of Sunbeam motor cycles, even although the work might conceivably be done without them. In this connection it may be mentioned that although a particular operation can be carried out without the use of special tools, the fact that the makers have designed a tool for a particular purpose is in itself evidence that the use of this special tool effects a considerable saving of time or, alternatively, enables work to be done more efficiently.

SERVICE TOOLS FOR SUNBEAM MODELS

Description.	Comprising parts.	Part number.	Suitable for
Extractor for flywheel, layshaft coupling and worm-shaft flange coupling .	—	89–9100	All models
	Extractor body	89–9101	
	Jack screw *	89–9102	
Flywheel nut spanner and tommy bar .	—	89–9103	,,
Valve-spring compressor . .	—	89–9104	,,
Clutch assembly (complete) . .	—	89–9109	,,
	Jack screw *	89–9102	
	Spider	89–9110	
	Cross member attachment	89–9111	
	Stems with tommy bars, 2 per set each	89–9111 / 89–9112	
	Circlips, 2 per set each	89–9115	
Rear suspension dismantling and assembly tool . .	—	61–3222	,,
Fork-leg extractor .	—	61–3009	,,
Fork top nut spanner	—	61–3001	S8 only
Fork oil-seal holder tool . . .	—	61–3005	
Fork oil-seal extractor	—	61–3006	
Fork oil-seal assembly tool . . .	—	61–3007	
Fork-leg bottom nut spanner . .	—	61–3003	
Fork-leg assembly tool . . .	—	61–3076	

* This tool is common to both 89–9100 and 89–9109.

METRIC AND DECIMAL EQUIVALENTS

Inches.		Mm.	Inches.		Mm.
$\frac{1}{64}$	0·016	0·396	$\frac{33}{64}$	0·516	13·096
$\frac{1}{32}$	0·031	0·793	$\frac{17}{32}$	0·531	13·492
$\frac{3}{64}$	0·047	1·190	$\frac{35}{64}$	0·547	13·890
$\frac{1}{16}$	0·063	1·587	$\frac{9}{16}$	0·563	14·287
$\frac{5}{64}$	0·078	1·984	$\frac{37}{64}$	0·578	14·683
$\frac{3}{32}$	0·094	2·381	$\frac{19}{32}$	0·594	15·080
$\frac{7}{64}$	0·109	2·778	$\frac{39}{64}$	0·609	15·477
$\frac{1}{8}$	0·125	3·175	$\frac{5}{8}$	0·625	15·875
$\frac{9}{64}$	0·141	3·571	$\frac{41}{64}$	0·641	16·271
$\frac{5}{32}$	0·156	3·968	$\frac{21}{32}$	0·656	16·667
$\frac{11}{64}$	0·172	4·365	$\frac{43}{64}$	0·672	17·064
$\frac{3}{16}$	0·188	4·762	$\frac{11}{16}$	0·688	17·462
$\frac{13}{64}$	0·203	5·159	$\frac{45}{64}$	0·703	17·858
$\frac{7}{32}$	0·219	5·556	$\frac{23}{32}$	0·719	18·255
$\frac{15}{64}$	0·234	5·953	$\frac{47}{64}$	0·734	18·652
$\frac{1}{4}$	0·25	6·350	$\frac{3}{4}$	0·75	19·050
$\frac{17}{64}$	0·266	6·746	$\frac{49}{64}$	0·766	19·446
$\frac{9}{32}$	0·281	7·143	$\frac{25}{32}$	0·781	19·842
$\frac{19}{64}$	0·297	7·540	$\frac{51}{64}$	0·797	20·239
$\frac{5}{16}$	0·313	7·937	$\frac{13}{16}$	0·813	20·637
$\frac{21}{64}$	0·328	8·334	$\frac{53}{64}$	0·828	21·033
$\frac{11}{32}$	0·344	8·730	$\frac{27}{32}$	0·844	21·429
$\frac{23}{64}$	0·359	9·127	$\frac{55}{64}$	0·859	21·827
$\frac{3}{8}$	0·375	9·525	$\frac{7}{8}$	0·875	22·225
$\frac{25}{64}$	0·391	9·921	$\frac{57}{64}$	0·891	22·621
$\frac{13}{32}$	0·406	10·318	$\frac{29}{32}$	0·906	23·017
$\frac{27}{64}$	0·422	10·715	$\frac{59}{64}$	0·922	23·414
$\frac{7}{16}$	0·438	11·112	$\frac{15}{16}$	0·938	23·812
$\frac{29}{64}$	0·453	11·508	$\frac{61}{64}$	0·953	24·208
$\frac{15}{32}$	0·469	11·905	$\frac{31}{32}$	0·969	24·604
$\frac{31}{64}$	0·484	12·302	$\frac{63}{64}$	0·984	25·002
$\frac{1}{2}$	0·5	12·700			

SCREW THREADS

Size (in.)	Whitworth			B.S.F.		
	T.P.I.	Core Diam. (in.)	Tap Drill	T.P.I.	Core Diam. (in.)	Tap Drill
	40	0·093	39	—	—	—
	24	0·1341	64 in.	—	0·2007	—
	20	0·1680	10	26	0·2320	B
	—	—	—	26	0·2543	G
	18	0·2414	D	22	0·3110	O
	16	0·2950	S	20	0·3664	U
	14	0·3460	in.	18	0·4200	in.
	12	0·3933	in.	16	0·4825	in.
	12	0·4558	in.	16	0·5335	in.
	11	0·5086	in.	14	0·5960	in.
	11	0·5711	in.	14	0·6433	in.
	10	0·6219	in.	12	0·7586	in.
	9	0·7327	in.	11	0·8719	in.
	8	0·8399	in.	10		in.

British Association (B.A.).

	0	1	2	3	4	5	6	7	8	9	10
T.P.I.	25·4	28·2	31·4	34·8	38·5	43·0	47·9	52·9	59·1	65·1	72·6
Ext. diam. (in.)	0·2362	0·2087	0·1850	0·1614	0·1417	0·1260	0·1102	0·0984	0·0866	0·0784	0·0669
Core diam. (in.)	0·1890	0·1661	0·1468	0·1269	0·1106	0·0981	0·0852	0·0758	0·0663	0·0564	0·0504
Tap drill	10	17	24	29	32	37	43	46	50	53	54

INDEX

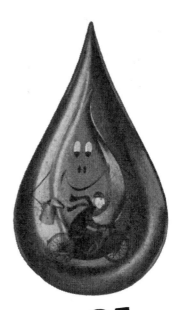

The makers of the

recommend

LONDON & HOME COUNTIES

MIDLAND COUNTIES

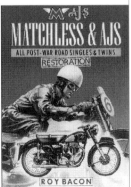

For top quality Classic and Vintage Motorcycle Manuals
See our web sites
www.classicmotorcyclemanuals.com
www.bsamanuals.com

or contact Steve Brown
steve@bsamanuals.com
0191 435 4122

For top quality Classic and Vintage Motorcycle Manuals
See our web sites
www.classicmotorcyclemanuals.com
www.bsamanuals.com

or contact Steve Brown
steve@bsamanuals.com
0191 435 4122